Elephants and Ivories

LOS ANGELES COUNTY MUSEUM OF ART

Elephants and Ivories in South Asia

Pratapaditya Pal

Published by the
Los Angeles County Museum of Art
5905 Wilshire Boulevard
Los Angeles, California 90036

Copyright © 1981 by
Museum Associates of the
Los Angeles County Museum of Art

Designed by Coy Los Angeles

Text set in Zapf International Light
with headings in Baldur by
RS Typographics, Los Angeles

Printed in an edition of 15,000 on
Karma Text by George Rice & Sons,
Los Angeles

Library of Congress Cataloging in Publication Data

Pal, Pratapaditya

  Elephants and ivories in South Asia.
  Bibliography: p.
  1. Arts—South Asia. 2. Elephants in art.
3. Elephants in literature. 4. Ivories—South Asia.
I. Los Angeles County Museum of Art. II. Title.
NX575.8.P3   700′.954′074019493   81–17980
ISBN 0–87587–105–4   AACR2

Table of Contents

Preface

This book is a new departure for the Museum since it replaces the catalogue that usually accompanies an exhibition. Although the scope of the book is determined by the limitations of the exhibition, it is hoped that this publication will attract a wider readership and will have a more general value than a catalogue. A checklist at the back, however, should serve those who are specifically interested in catalogue information about the individual objects.

The book is also restricted by the fact that, by and large, our choice has been confined to objects in the collection. In order to fill the lacunae in the Museum's holdings, however, we have secured several loans, mostly from local collectors. It is a great pleasure to record my deep appreciation to these generous lenders who are identified in the checklist that also serves as the list of illustrations. Their beautiful objects have certainly enhanced the quality of the exhibition and the book.

A project such as this cannot be accomplished without the cooperation of the entire staff of the Museum. It is a pleasure for me to thank all of them. A few individuals, however, have gone out of their way to render special assistance. By naming them here, I have no intention of neglecting others: Ebria Feinblatt, Bruce Davis, and George Kuwayama; Sheila Sklar, Jaleh Ghobad, and Robert Brown of the Indian Art Department; Jeanne D'Andrea and Ann Koepfli for their editorial help; and Larry Reynolds for photography.

The book is written for the general public rather than the specialist; diacritical marks on the Indian words, therefore, have not been used. In presenting this modest publication no one is more aware than the author of how inexhaustible the subject is. It is hoped that the book will serve merely as an *hors d'oeuvre* and that some day a more sumptuous and substantial main course will follow.

Pratapaditya Pal

6

Introduction

It was six men of Indostan
To learning much inclined,
Who went to see the Elephant
(Though all of them were blind),
That each by observation
Might satisfy his mind.

The First approached the Elephant,
And happening to fall
Against his broad and sturdy side,
At once began to bawl:
'God bless me! but the Elephant
Is very like a wall!'

The Second, feeling of the tusk,
Cried, 'Ho! what have we here
So very round and smooth and sharp?
To me 'tis mighty clear
This wonder of an Elephant
Is very like a spear!'

The Third approached the animal,
And happening to take
The squirming trunk within his hands,
Thus boldly up and spake:
'I see,' quoth he, 'the Elephant
Is very like a snake.'

The Fourth reached out his eager hand,
And felt about the knee.
'What most this wondrous beast is like
Is mightily plain,' quoth he;
''Tis clear enough the Elephant
Is very like a tree!'

The Fifth, who chanced to touch the ear,
Said: 'E'en the blindest man
Can tell what this resembles most:
Deny the fact who can,
This marvel of an Elephant
Is very like a fan!'

The Sixth no sooner had begun
About the beast to grope,
Than, seizing on the swinging tail
That fell within his scope,
'I see,' quoth he, 'the Elephant
Is very like a rope!'

And so these men of Indostan
Disputed loud and long,
Each in his own opinion
Exceeding stiff and strong,
Though each was partly in the right,
And all were in the wrong!

John Godfrey Saxe
1877–1953

8

No other poem has painted a more humorous picture of the outrageously curious shape of the elephant than the above adaptation of an Indian fable. Strange and fascinating, the elephant is also a vivid reminder of those early days when giant creatures of many sorts roamed the earth (1). Large and ponderous, a juggernaut when wild but friendly when tamed, the elephant, along with the bull and the buffalo, has remained as close to man in South Asia as the horse once was to Europeans and Americans. It is no wonder that the elephant figures so prominently in both the myths and arts of South Asia which, with Africa, is one of the two remaining habitats of this mammoth. In South Asia the elephant is found today on the Indian subcontinent, on the island of Sri Lanka, in the Himalayan kingdom of Nepal, and in most countries of Southeast Asia.

9

2. *Elephant*
India, Rajput Style, Kotah School, 18th century

3. *A Snake Goddess Riding an Elephant*
Tibet, 18th century

Despite the inventions of modern science, the elephant is still the "prime mover" of heavy burdens in South Asia. The animal may be considered nature's forklift, and one can often see elephants in Asian villages moving enormous weights, such as logs, large boulders, and so forth, with that remarkable part of its anatomy, the trunk (2). It is this extraordinary limb that has provided the most common name for the animal in India (*hasti* or *hathi*, derived from the words *hasta* or *hath*, meaning arm). The fact that the Indians have always loved this animal, however, is evident from the many different names given to it in Sanskrit. Among the more interesting is *naga*, a word which is also used for both mountain and a snake. The association of the elephant and the serpent is clearly expressed in a Tibetan bronze of a snake-goddess *(nagini)* riding an elephant (3).

The elephant's bulk immediately brings to mind a mountain, yet because of its trunk, one of the blind men in the poem quoted above mistook it for a snake. In fact, the trunk of the elephant is perhaps its most fascinating limb. Originally it was called a trump, from the French *trompe* meaning a trumpet, but trump somehow became confused with the word trunk. When an elephant calls, it raises its trunk in a heraldic manner and does indeed trumpet, and in medieval European renderings of the animal the trunk is often drawn like a trumpet. Well over two thousand years ago a Chinese gentleman was so intrigued by the animal

that he wrote: "When we look at him from the front, we think we are looking at his posterior because he has a trunk which looks like his tail. When he walks it is, as it were, as if a mountain moved, but ah, how hard to know whether he is coming or going!" In the same vein, Hilaire Belloc penned the following equally amusing lines:

When people call this beast to mind,
They marvel more and more
At such a LITTLE tail behind
So LARGE a trunk before.

The English word elephant comes from the Greek *elephas*, perhaps derived either from the Sanskrit *ibha* through the Arabic *al-ipha* or from the Indo-Iranian *pil* through the Arabic *al-fil*. In any event, both the Greeks and the Romans were familiar with the elephant, and we all know that Hannibal (1st century B.C.) successfully crossed the Alps with the help of elephants that appear to have been Indian. This brings me to the second great use of the elephant: it was the amphibian tank of the ancient world. An elephant brigade was as important in the Indian army as the cavalry, and kings often fought from the elephant's back. The Indian king Porus, the legendary hero who made Alexander turn back from the banks of the river Hydaspes in the Panjab, faced the Macedonian from his elephant. Each king had his favorite elephants, and there are many pictures of the great Mughal Emperor Akbar (16th cen-

tury) fighting and hunting from the back of one of his four thousand elephants (4). Akbar's court historian, Abul Fazal, has left us a lengthy and vivid account of the elephant, and the following passage reveals how useful it was in battle:

This wonderful animal is in bulk and strength like a mountain; and in courage and ferocity like a lion. It adds materially to the pomp of a king and to the success of a conqueror; and is of the greatest use for the army. Experienced men of Hindustan put the value of a good elephant equal to five hundred horses; and they believe, that when guided by a few bold men armed with matchlocks, such an elephant alone is worth double that number (5).

Like a modern tank the elephant's progress is slow but sure. A confident swimmer, it can also negotiate difficult terrain and clear a path through thickets and jungles by snapping branches as we would match sticks and by uprooting trees. Rudyard Kipling, perhaps the greatest writer of elephant stories, eloquently expressed this power:

The torn boughs tailing o'er the tusks aslant,
The saplings reeling in the path he trod,
Declare his might—our lord The Elephant,
Chief of the ways of God.

The elephant was also used in ancient warfare as a battering-ram. Perhaps the most graphic description of this occurs in the Buddhist chronicle of Sri Lanka, called the

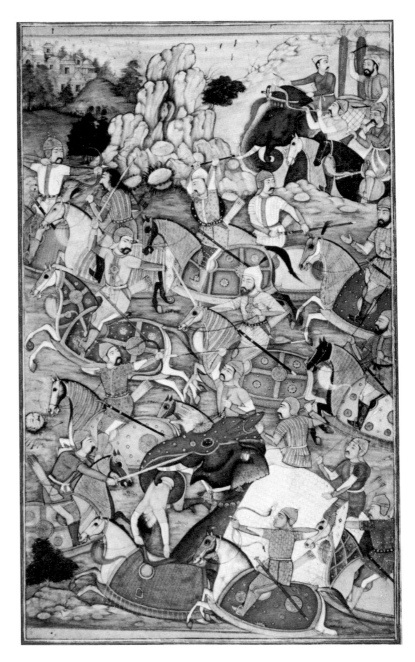

13

Mahavamsa, compiled about the fifth century A.D. The account also reveals how close the elephant was to man and how well they communicated with each other, almost on a mystic level. When Dutthagamani, the king of Sri Lanka, besieged the city of his enemies, the fortress, with its gates of wrought iron, seemed impregnable. The king, however, let loose his most powerful elephant called Kandula, "Placing himself upon his knees and battering stones, mortar and bricks with his tusks did the elephant attack the gate of iron." The enemy then poured molten pitch upon the animal who, tormented with pain, dived into a pool.

The elephant's physician washed the pitch away and put on balm; the king mounted the elephant and, stroking his temple with his hand, he cheered him on with the words: "To thee I give, dear Kandula, the lordship over the whole island of Lanka." And when he had had choice fodder given to him, had covered him with a cloth and had put his armour on him and had bound upon his skin a seven-times-folded buffalo hide and above it had laid a hide steeped in oil he set him free. Roaring like thunder he came, daring danger, and with his tusks pierced the panels of the gate and trampled the threshold with his feet; and with uproar the gate

crashed to the ground together with the arches of the gate.

Battlefields, however, are not the only place where the elephant displays his worth and usefulness. As elsewhere in the world, hunting in India was a favorite sport of the princes and nobility. On a gold coin of the Gupta emperor, Kumaragupta I (c. 415–455), we see him hunting a lion from the security of an elephant's back (6). In much the same way, an eighteenth-century Rajput prince and his elephant attack a tiger in a vigorously drawn picture of the Kotah school (7). For sheer pomp and ceremony, no sight is more impressive than a procession of gaily caparisoned elephants. The subject was very popular with artists in India and we repeatedly encounter princes and their spouses riding majestic elephants, such as we see in a charming little South Indian bronze (8). More formal and ceremonious is the Persian prince who rides in state on a spotted elephant in a thirteenth-century Minai bowl (9). Elephants also served as state executioners and were sometimes called upon to gouge and trample a condemned man to death.

The most generous contribution of this extraordinary creature is his tusk, though the loss is involuntary and tragic. The elephant is perhaps the only animal that helps man to hunt and is also hunted by man. Elephant hunting was a favorite sport (10) with the maharajas of India, and, later, with their British masters. An enormous quantity of royal furniture was made entirely of ivory, and we can imagine the number of tusks that were

necessary to manufacture the various thrones, chairs, and cabinets of just a single palace. Some idea can be formed from the following account left us by the eighteenth-century Dutchman, François Valentijn. Writing about elephant hunts in Sri Lanka, he says:

> In former times there were large elephant hunts but the Governor Simons has in his time begun the capture of elephants in small *kraals* [corrals] with much profit.... From August 1707 till the 31st October...62 beasts were captured without significant expense....

If a haul of sixty-two elephants in a short period of three months on one small island is considered a small hunt, one wonders what a large hunt must have been like.

Ivory, in fact, gave the elephant its name, for the Greek *elephas* originally meant ivory, and the prehistoric mastodon is also named for its enormous molars. Elephant tusks have been prized since man's first hunting days, and ivory continues to be used extensively for making jewelry, furnishings, combs, and for sculpture—both secular and religious. The ivories illustrated and discussed here give only a very general idea of the many ways in which this material is used in South Asia. Since antiquity, it has been carved with great imagination and skill by craftsmen in Europe and West Asia as well. Because African ivory is preferred for carving, Indian merchants have imported large quantities to help satisfy the desire for ivory products.

Strong demand and limited supply have made ivory an expensive commodity, and undoubtedly inspired the Bengali adage that even a dead elephant is worth a million rupees. Thus, only rich merchants, royalty, or affluent religious establishments could afford to buy the beautiful ivory objects illustrated here.

A few words must also be said about the nature of the elephant. While it looks formidable and has its menacing moments, by and large the tame Indian elephant is a gentle and amiable animal, as everyone who has been to a zoo or a circus knows. Once again we turn to Abul Fazal for a graphic picture of the elephant's character and personality:

> In vehemence on one side, and submissiveness to the reins on the other, the elephant is like an Arab, whilst in point of obedience and attentiveness to even the slightest signs, it resembles an intelligent human being. In restiveness when full-blooded, and in vindictiveness, it surpasses man.

While one may doubt the truth of this last observation, the elephant is remarkably like a human in many other respects. Both the male and the female of the species are extremely tender and loving toward their young. Female elephants are said to fast, waste away, and sometimes even die of grief, when mourning the loss of their calves. Abul Fazal records two touching anecdotes about the intelligence as well as the filial devotion of the elephant. He had heard both anecdotes from the emperor Akbar himself. Once a wild calf who had fallen into a pit was

left there for the night. When the emperor visited the pit in the morning, he found to his amazement that during the night "some wild elephants had filled the pit with broken logs and grass, and thus pulled out the young one." The second story is about the elephant who, when captured, feigned death. "We passed her, and went onwards; but when at night we returned we saw no trace left of her."

Stories of rogue elephants are well known and even the most courageous hunter will shrink from encounters with a herd of wild elephants. In the great Indian epic, the *Mahabharata*, we are given a vivid account of the devastation that a herd of elephants caused to a caravan of merchants camped beside a lake (11). In the middle of the night when everyone was fast asleep, the elephants arrived to drink water. Seeing the caravan obstruct their path, the herd:

> ...trampled the sleeping people, who lay suddenly writhing on the ground. Screaming, the merchants tried to find shelter and, still blind from sleep, dived into the bushes to escape the grave danger. Some were killed by tusks and trunks, others trampled underfoot. The whole panic-stricken caravan with its men, bullocks, donkeys, camels and horses mixed with travellers on foot took to flight, crowding one another. Uttering fearful cries they fell on the ground, clutched at trees with broken limbs, or stumbled into trenches; and so that whole rich caravan camp was struck down.

The entire description sounds as if the camp were struck by a hurricane. No wonder Indian poets compared the elephant with mountains and menacing monsoon clouds. One also wonders whether the creators of the Hollywood film *The Elephant Walk* had read the above account before shooting that memorable scene in Sri Lanka when the British teaplanter (Peter Finch) refused to allow a herd of thirsty elephants to go through his plantation to drink water. The dire results were predictable.

Strict vegetarians, elephants thrive on fruits, leaves, and often entire trees, particularly bananas. Herds of elephants are known to go through groves of banana trees in one night just as a group of children might devour an entire candy shop if given the opportunity. Elephants also love water in which they frolic with much greater mirth than the hippo and the water-buffalo. There will be more about this trait in a later chapter.

The remarkable intelligence and memory of elephants are proverbial. As the classical scholar Arrian (2nd century) says in his *Indika*, "The elephant is of all brutes the most intelligent. Some of them, for instance, have taken up their riders when slain in battle and carried them away for burial; others have covered them, when lying on the ground, with a shield; and others have borne the brunt of battle in their defense when fallen." Those of us who have been to the circus know how well elephants perform, and they have done so for centuries. Once again Arrian writes:

21

I have myself actually seen an elephant playing on cymbals, while other elephants were dancing to his strains: a cymbal had been attached to each foreleg of the performer, and a third to what is called his trunk, and while he beat in turn the cymbal on his trunk he beat in proper time those on his two legs. The dancing elephants all the while kept dancing in a circle, and as they raised and curved their forelegs in turn they too moved in proper time, following as the musicians led.

Stories and anecdotes also abound about their exceptional retentive powers, some of which must have inspired Dorothy Parker to write somewhat cynically in her *Ballade of Unfortunate Mammals:*

Prince, a precept I leave for you,
Coined in Eden, existing yet:
Skirt the parlor, and shun the zoo—
Women and elephants never forget.

The Elephant in Mythology and Literature

In the forest the lord of the kingdom saw
Great herds of grand elephants, leaders of herds,
That were flowing with rut and stood like mountains,
Together with a herd of elephant cows.

Mahabharata

Eh pietate virum insignem, virtute decorum,
Clementé Stephanú, placidúq; hilaréq; benignú,
Munificum supra quàm dici possit in omneis:

Nam moriturus constanter precibus, sceleratis
Pro hostibus, orabat Dominum vultuq; sereno,
Vno in quo fixit sibi Spem, metamq; salutis.

Animals play a very important role in Indian religion, mythology, and literature, and it is not surprising to find that the elephant is a star in many legends. One of the most popular and important gods of India is Ganesa, the elephant-headed deity, who will be discussed later. This chapter will present some of the fascinating myths that have developed around the elephant and its use in literature as both symbol and metaphor.

The earliest Indian religious literature, known as the Vedas, was compiled by the priestly members of a people now known as Aryans. It is generally believed that these Aryans, belonging to the broader Indo-European family, moved into India sometime about 1500 B.C., and that the Vedas were composed shortly thereafter, certainly no later than 700 B.C. Long before the arrival of the Aryans, the elephant had been domesticated in South Asia. It figures prominently on seals excavated at various sites associated with the Indus Valley civilization—the earliest (c. 2500 B.C.) on the subcontinent. One can well imagine the incredulity and amazement of the first Aryans, nevertheless, when they encountered the elephant, perhaps in the Panjab. Certainly, their admiration for the voracious appetite as well as the strength and majesty of the elephant is expressed clearly in Vedic poems. How appropriate is the following comparison of the Vedic storm-gods, the Maruts, with the elephants:

Mighty, with wondrous power and marvellously bright, self-strong like mountains, ye glide swiftly on your way.

Like the wild elephants ye eat the forests up when ye assume your strength among the bright red flames.

Frequently in Indian literature elephants are associated with clouds, no doubt due to color and rounded shape, and also because of the manner in which they can spray water from their trunks. Furthermore, after the myth arose that elephants could fly, they were sometimes portrayed with wings. The symbol of the elephant as a mountain-top or cloud may have contributed to its association with the axis of the universe, and it has been suggested that this idea may have led to the use of the elephant in the Middle Ages in Europe "as an emblem of wisdom, of moderation, of eternity, and also of piety." Perhaps this explains why St. Stephen is seen riding an elephant in the sixteenth-century engraving by the Dutch artist Coornhert (13).

In Indian art, however, the association of the elephant with clouds is more direct. In a painting representing the month of Bhadoh (August–September when the monsoons are at their most menacing) the herds of excited elephants rampaging in a tropical jungle are as ominous as the clouds above (11). More amusing is the picture in which, quite unconcerned with laws of nature, the artist has placed an elephant on the roof and the rains come down like a curtain of beads (14).

In addition to other symbolic relationships, an unknown Aryan poet has associated the splendor of the elephant with the cosmic splendor of man:

May the splendor of an elephant, the greatest of all creatures,
may that great glory,
which was born from the Boundless, now be diffused.
The Gods together have bestowed it upon me.

***

That splendor that resides in an elephant, in a king
among men, or within the waters,
with which the Gods in the beginning came to godhood,
with that same splendor make me splendid, O Lord.

***

From the four directions, as far the eye
can direct its gaze,
may that force, that elephant splendor, assemble
and concentrate its virtue in me.
Behold the elephant, best of all creatures
to mount and to ride!
I anoint myself with his share of strength,
with his elephant splendor.

This remarkably evocative poem is not merely an ecstatic exalta-
tion of the elephant but provides us with interesting clues as to
its function in Aryan society. The Aryans came into India riding
horses and were primarily horsemen and charioteers. How
quickly they must have recognized the symbolic value of the
elephant as an appropriate mount for kings. Indeed, few sights
are as impressive and as indicative of the pomp and might of
an oriental monarch as a king riding a caparisoned elephant
and looking down from his royal height at his subjects. The
symbolic value of a ruler riding in state on an elephant was
recognized by the British too after they assumed absolute politi-
cal power in India during the reign of Queen Victoria. She may
have been the empress of India, but her state rides in London,
even in a gilded coach, could hardly match the splendor of her
viceroy riding an elephant in India. That the Vedic Aryans had
quickly appreciated the emblematic power of the majestic
elephant is evident from the expression "best of all creatures to
mount and to ride" in the poem above.

Even more important is the fact that the poet should have
found in the animal an appropriate metaphor to express the
cosmic splendor of man. The poem beautifully expresses a very
fundamental element of the Vedic tradition: "Human plenitude
is not attained by isolation from the rest of the world, nor does
it consist in the development of one part of the human being.
Man integrates in himself all the realms of the world and he
radiates the splendor of the entire universe." The poem also
demonstrates the sense of awe that this animal instilled in
Vedic man, for its glorification by the author becomes almost
excessive praise. It is obvious that man is here seeking the
splendor of the animal world symbolized by the elephant. One
wonders if Kenneth Clark is not correct in questioning the tra-

वोरतघनचरूरोरोष्‍निर्घर्घनिमंडहि ॥ घाराघरघरघरनिमुस
लधारनिजलुछंडहि ॥ झिल्‍लीगानझंकारपवनमुकिमुकिअकझक
ञारत ॥ सिंचवाचगुंजरतऊजुकुजरनउतोरत ॥ निसिदिनविसब
निःसबमतिकंतझंबोडोवोउिए ॥ दसपयूषविदसविष्‍णुसुनादोन्‍न
वनुनंछाडिएपद्‍ ॥

27

ditional interpretation of some prehistoric cave paintings. It is generally believed that these astonishingly powerful representations of animals were meant to give the hunter power over his victims through sympathetic magic. While Clark does not deny the validity of sympathetic magic for hunting tribes, with characteristic incisiveness, he asks:

> Can this be true of the lively, energetic animals that can be dimly discerned on the uneven walls of Altamira? The few men who appear in Lascaux cut very poor figures compared to the vigorous animals. Can we seriously believe that they thought they were gaining power over their magnificent companions? Are they not rather expressing their envy and admiration?

Indeed, if the Vedic Aryans who were far from simple hunters could express their ungrudging admiration for animals so late in history, how much more the primitive man?

In view of Vedic man's partiality to the elephant as a symbol of regal and cosmic splendor, it is natural that Indra, his chief god, should be given the animal as a mount (15). In later mythology Indra came to be regarded as *devaraja* or the king of gods and his elephant is called Airavata. At times, his elephant is a normal animal, but at others, as in a Rajput painting, it has five heads which symbolize the four directions and the center. A story about Indra tells how the gods and demons resorted to churning the ocean in a sort of tug-of-war to determine who

would be lord of the universe. Among various trophies that emerged from the ocean was the divine elephant Airavata which was coveted by Indra(16). By the time the legend of Airavata arrived in Thailand, the elephant had grown both in stature and cosmic splendor. Known as Airavana or Eravana, he now possessed thirty-three instead of five heads. The number thirty-three probably symbolizes the thirty-three heavens of the gods. Finally, in a Thai text called *The Three Worlds*, "the elephant became a veritable microcosm."

The emergence of the elephant from the ocean in the Indian myth narrated above reiterates the animal's association with water, fertility, and clouds which drop life-giving rains. Elaboration of this symbolism led to the concept of the Indian goddess of wealth and fortune being showered by four elephants representing the four directions (*dig-gaja*), as seen in a bronze from Orissa (only two are visible in the front view 17). In this emanation she is known as Gajalakshmi, and the elephants symbolize clouds as well as the directions.

The elephant is regarded as an auspicious symbol in both India and Southeast Asia, and often is worshiped directly (18). In Java there is a very early (c. A.D. 450) inscription carved on a rock: "[Here] shineth the pair of footprints of the . . . Airavata-like elephant of the lord of Taruma [who is] great in conquering . . ." On either side of the inscription are carved two enormous footprints of an elephant. In another early Javanese

inscription the island is described in paradisical terms. We are told that in Java

> …there is a wonderful place dedicated
> to Sambhu, a heaven of heavens,
> surrounded by the Ganges and other holy
> resorts and laid in a beautiful woodland
> inhabited by elephants, existing for
> the good of the world.

Of all animals, only elephants live in this heavenly place.

Both in Burma and Thailand the elephant is given an almost divine status, as was noted in the nineteenth century by Mrs. Anna Leonowens, the English governess to the children of the King of Siam. "From the earliest times," she wrote, "the kings of Siam and Birmah have anxiously sought for the white elephant, and having had the rare fortune to procure one, have loaded it with gifts and dignities, as though it were a conscious favourite of the throne." Brought to the capital, the elephant was then subjected to a ceremony in a pavilion of extraordinary splendor built for the occasion. The lavish ceremony rivaled a royal coronation or a presidential inauguration. Anna was present in 1862 when one such captured white elephant died before his ceremonial investiture in which the elephant is ritually anointed with consecrated water poured on his forehead. The grief-stricken king was consoled by his son who assured his royal father that the "stranger lord, fatally pampered, had

31

19. *King Vessantara Gives His White Elephant Away*
Thailand, 19th century

20. *Vishnu Rescues Gajendra, the Elephant King*
India, Rajput Style, Kotah School, c. 1825

succumbed to astonishment and indigestion."

The belief in the auspiciousness of the white elephant is very old in India. The Vedic god Indra's elephant is white and the Buddha was conceived by his mother as a white elephant. In another immensely popular Buddhist myth we are told that in one of his previous lives the Buddha was born as Vessantara, the king of Sibi. A compulsively generous man, he gave away his state elephant, which was white, to a neighboring kingdom suffering from a severe drought (19). The white elephant was believed to possess the magical power to cause rain. Undoubtedly, this is why the white elephant came to be regarded as a precious creature in Thailand and why the king was so disconsolate when a captured specimen died.

In the Hindu pantheon the elephant serves as the mount of the Great Goddess in her manifestation as Jagaddhatri or the "Sustainer of the Universe," and in one of the most popular myths represented in Indian art, Vishnu saved Gajendra, the "king of the elephants," when he was attacked by an alligator. As he was sporting in a lotus pond, Gajendra was attacked and called for Vishnu who immediately appeared and saved him (20).

This is, of course, an edifying myth invented by the Vaishavas to demonstrate the power of faith.

Among the Jainas the elephant serves as the mount of at least two Yakshas when they act as attendants of the gods, but curiously is not associated with any of the Jinas, the emancipated teachers who are the principal personages venerated by the Jainas. The Jainas, however, do regard the elephant as an auspicious symbol (21). In the legendary life story of the greatest Jaina teacher, Mahavira (6th century B.C.), we are told that before his birth, his mother had a dream in which she saw the fourteen auspicious symbols, including the elephant, all of which gave a divine character to the birth.

The elephant plays a more direct role in the story of the

birth of another great religious figure in India. According to tradition, Siddhartha, better known as the Buddha, was conceived by his mother as a white elephant. In other words, the embryo entered Maya's womb in the form of an elephant. Buddhist mythology, furthermore, includes many other stories in which the elephant is the hero. Perhaps the best known and poignant is the story of one of the Buddha's previous lives as a white elephant whose six tusks emitted magical rays. Like all Indians the Buddhists believe in the theory of rebirth, and, before his last appearance on earth as Siddhartha when he was finally liberated, the Buddha had many previous lives. In one, the Buddha was the chief of a herd of elephants living in the Himalayas. His two favorite queens were Mahasubhadda and Chullasubhadda, and one day when all three were disporting themselves in a grove of trees, the chief shook some flowering branches. Because of the direction of the prevailing wind, the flowers fell on Mahasubhadda, the senior wife, and some twigs on Chullasubhadda. Offended, Chullasubhadda thought the chief favored the senior wife. On a second occasion, while dallying in a lotus pond, the elephant chief offered a beautiful flower

to his senior queen. Once again Chullasubhadda was offended and she soon began to waste away. She finally died, but not before asking the gods to be reborn in order to seek vengeance.

Reborn as Subhadda, she became the favorite queen of the king of Kasi. One day she told the king about the magical properties of the six tusks of her former husband whereupon the king ordered his hunters to kill the elephant chief and bring the tusks to his queen. The best hunter of the kingdom set off for the Himalayas and upon locating the chief struck him with a poisoned arrow. The wounded chief asked the hunter: "Why did you wound me? Was it for your own advantage or were you suborned by some one else?" The hunter then told him about the queen, wherupon the elephant chief said:

Rise, hunter, and ere I die,

Saw off these tusks of ivory:
Go bid the shrew be of good cheer,
The beast is slain; his tusks are here.

The hunter sawed off the tusks and brought them to the Queen of Kasi. On seeing the tusks the queen cried: "Do you tell me that he is dead?" When the hunter's reply was affirmative, she placed the tusks on her lap and gazed at them for a while. Then, remembering her former husband, she realized her wickedness and was filled with such sorrow and remorse that she died that very day of a broken heart. The story has inspired some of the finest representations in early Buddhist art.

Indian mythology, however, has not always presented the elephant in so favorable a light. In keeping with the widespread Indian belief that good and evil exist together in every being, whether mortal or immortal, human or animal, the elephant is often seen as an adversary, especially the rogue elephant. Thus, there is the story of the divine child Krishna who destroyed the elephant-demon Kuvalayapida, sent by Krishna's wicked uncle Kamsa to kill the boy (22). In a charming eighteenth-century Himalayan painting, we encounter the goddess Durga dispatching an elephant, as well as a buffalo and a lion (23). Apparently, in order to delude the goddess, the demon Mahishasura had assumed various shapes, one of which was the elephant. Equally well known is the story of Siva's destruction of the elephant demon Gajasura, whose flayed skin the god always

35

wears as a mantle.

The elephant also figures as an adversary in the legendary life stories of both the Buddha and Mahavira. Devadatta, the Buddha's jealous cousin and spiritual rival, let loose the mad elephant Nalagiri to destroy the Master (12). In keeping with the pacific nature of the Buddha's doctrine, however, he did not kill the animal in a bloody encounter as the Hindu deities did but, instead, subdued him with kindness. This incident has come to be regarded as one of the eight principal events or miracles of the Buddha's life, and we see it represented here in an eleventh-century manuscript illumination (24).

Mahavira's confrontation with a rogue elephant is graphically narrated by the great Jaina author Hemachandra Suri (11th century). Here Mahavira's antagonist is an evil god named Sangamaka. As Mahavira was about to reach enlightenment, Sangamaka tried in vain to distract him with both violent and seductive means. The evil god created and let loose an angry elephant:

He ran forward, bending the earth,
as it were, with his uplifted trunk.
The elephant seized the Blessed One
with the end of his trunk hard to
resist and tossed him high up in the air.
Thinking, "He, [Mahavira] shattered, has gone to pieces,"
pitiless, he [the elephant] received him falling from the air,

raising his tusks. When he [Mahavira] had fallen, he wounded him again and again by blows with his tusks and sparks flew up from the diamond-hard breast [of the Lord]. When the rogue-elephant was not able to do anything, the god created a female elephant like a female enemy. But she too failed and was reduced to dust.

The use of the elephant as a simile or metaphor in secular literature is as rich as it is in mythology. Traditionally, Indian legends divide women into various classes and one of them is described as *hastini* or cow-elephant. One of the commonest compliments that an ancient Indian could pay to a woman with a graceful gait was to address her as *gajendra-gamini* or one who walks like an elephant. This may sound offensive to the ears of a modern woman, but for its enormous weight the elephant has a very rhythmic and poised walk. For those familiar with the Indian's love of well-endowed female forms in sculpture, the comparison is not entirely inappropriate.

In addition, Indian poets often compare certain limbs of the elephant with a woman's form, and the similarities have served as verbal models for the artist as well. Thus, a woman's breasts are compared with the two bumps on the elephant's forehead in the following verse by the poet Bhagura:

Your breasts, oh slender maid,
resemble an elephant's cranial lobes.
You are, as it were, a pool

37

shaken by the elephant, Youth, who plunges therein.
It is also very common to compare the shape of a woman's leg with the trunk of an elephant or the stem of a banana tree. Kalidasa (c. A.D. 400), however, the greatest of Sanskrit poets, disagreed with this comparison. While describing the physical charms of the goddess Parvati, he writes:

Usually poets compare the thigh of a woman with the trunk of an elephant or a banana tree. But Parvati's thighs cannot be compared with either for the skin of an elephant's trunk is too rough and the banana stem is cold and unexciting.

Kalidasa appears to have been particularly fond of using the elephant as a poetic simile. In his well-known work called the *Meghaduta* or the Cloud-messenger, which is a poem of only 115 verses, he has used the elephant (including its ichor and ivory) nine times. The poem is about a banished lover who pines away for his wife. One day he sees a cloud floating across the skies and sends through it a message of his loneliness and love to his young wife. In the second verse of the poem, Kalidasa strikes a beautiful simile when he describes the cloud "swelling against the peak like a great elephant nuzzling a hill." He warns the cloud-messenger to avoid "the proudly lifted trunks of the elephant guards of the eight directions." In a third verse, he compares the marks left by the waters of the river Reva on Vindhya's rocky side with "painted streaks upon an elephant's dingy hide."

Sanskrit was not the only language that used the elephant as a poetic metaphor. The early Tamil poets were equally fond of this native creature. The following is taken from the *Kuruntokai*, an anthology of love poems composed between A.D. 100–300. Written by the poet Kapilar, it is about a peasant maiden and is a beautiful example of "condensed poetic imagery and compact meaning," essential characteristics of such poems.

Does that girl
   eyes like flowers, gathering flowers
from pools for her garlands, driving away the parrots
From the millet fields,
   does that girl know at all
or doesn't she,
   that my heart is still there with her
   bellowing sighs
like a drowsy midnight elephant?

One of the *Jatakas*, edifying stories of the Buddha's previous lives in which he often assumed animal form, has been narrated earlier. Many other tales involving animals, however, are purely secular and are among the most popular fables of ancient India. The *Panchatantra* is one such collection of charming fables in which the animals themselves play the roles. Already translated into Persian and Chinese before the sixth century, their appeal is universal and versions of the stories have

been included in *The Arabian Nights* as well as in Medieval and Renaissance fables such as the *Decameron, Canterbury Tales, Reineke Fuchs, Fabliaux, Fables of La Fontaine*, and tales by the Brothers Grimm and Andersen. One of the fables in the *Panchatantra* is the story about elephants and mice in a lakeside town that had fallen into decay. The mice lived happily in the deserted town until the day a herd of elephants arrived in search of water. As they marched through the community of mice they crushed everything in their path. The few mice who managed to survive decided that they must appease the elephants, for they remembered the following adage:

An elephant will kill you if

He touch; a serpent if he sniff;

King's laughter has a deadly sting;

A rascal kills by honouring.

Appealing for their lives, they reminded the elephant king "that even creatures of our size will some day prove of service." The king realized the wisdom of this good counsel and changed his course.

Sometime later most of the elephants were trapped by royal hunters, brought to the capital, and tied up with ropes. The leader of the elephants then remembered the mice and sent for them at once. When they arrived, he reminded the mice of their promise and asked them to return the favor. The mice were only too glad to oblige and, by gnawing through the ropes,

set their friends free. One could hardly find a better story to demonstrate how to win friends and influence people.

The elephant itself is the subject of a vast body of literature in Sanskrit as well as in other languages of India and Southeast Asia. Not only are there numerous sections on the elephant in encyclopedic religious texts, but entirely separate texts known as *gaja-sastra* were compiled that discuss the origins, classifications, character, and diseases of the animal. Most foreign visitors to India, beginning with the Greek ambassador Megasthenes, had something to say about the elephant. Curiously, although the elephant has always played a much greater role in Indian civilization, the peacock rather than the elephant was chosen by independent India as the national emblem.

The health and welfare of the elephant was of paramount importance to Indian princes. Mentioned earlier was a special veterinarian in the retinue of King Dutthagamani of Sri Lanka. The Mughal emperor Akbar's historian Abul Fazal has also left us an extensive account of the huge staff that looked after the imperial elephants. Some of the veterinarian texts are richly illustrated and show different classifications of elephants and their afflictions. In an impressive eighteenth-century picture from Rajasthan, an artist has rendered with amusing explicitness an elephant being attacked by "fever" personified as a monster (25). Even though the multi-headed monster attacks ferociously, the elephant seems calm and undaunted.

The Elephant in Art

42

Elephants have always been popular motifs in the arts of South Asia and figure prominently in the painting and sculpture of the entire area. Throughout history they have been portrayed with remarkable dexterity by South Asian artists. By contrast, neither the Europeans (at least until Rembrandt) nor the Chinese quite succeeded in mastering the anatomy of this—to them—foreign creature. Since the animal was not native to either region (although South China did have a variety of elephants in pre-historic times) it is unlikely that more than a few artists ever saw a live elephant. Their depictions until recently, therefore, remained conceptual but not without charm and humor. In a sixteenth-century French print illustrating various animals, we see the elephant more as a menacing mammoth of pre-history (1) than the friendly creature whose trunk children love to stroke when they visit the zoo. Far more credible is the elephant carrying St. Stephen in the Dutch print of the same century (13); the artist must have seen a representation of a caparisoned animal in either an Iranian or an Indian picture. What is noteworthy is the delineation of the trunk by both European artists, for it is indeed more like a *trompe* than a trunk. The Chinese elephant carrying a Buddhist saint or Lohan (26) seems almost as belligerent as that in the French print, while the fine jade elephant is quite imaginative and amusing (27).

Whether in sculpture or in painting, the artists of South Asia have always represented the elephant with self-confidence

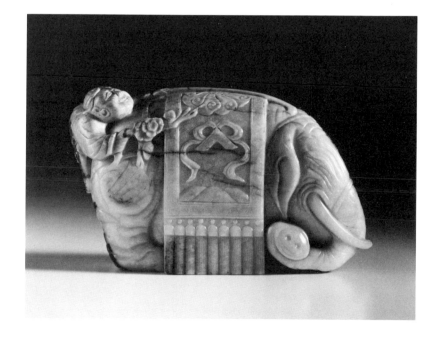

43

and empathy, but they have never been comfortable with the horse. On the other hand, how admirable are the great Greco-Roman sculptures of horses or those done in T'ang China. Close observation certainly had something to do with this, but Indian artists of all ages also had ample opportunity to observe horses. Yet, their representations rarely achieve the certainty and conviction that they display in delineating an elephant or a bull; there is nothing contrived in their representations of these animals, and, even if the forms are sometimes abstract, their essence and character are always conveyed with astonishing sensitivity.

Indian manuals of art provide detailed instructions for drawing an elephant. The artist is directed to make a grid of 120 squares and then draw an outline of the animal, but it is doubtful if such instructions were followed implicitly. Certainly, sculptors were less likely to use any grid, while the drawings and paintings illustrated here are executed so spontaneously and with such animation that the application of a grid seems unlikely (28). The only picture that may have been drawn following a grid pattern is the one in which we see the fever-demon attacking an elephant (25). It does seem, however, that most artists followed the instruction to start drawing only after acute observation.

The elephant figures prominently among the auspicious symbols that were used to decorate domestic buildings, whether they were palaces or humble peasant dwellings. If one visits Indian villages today, one often sees elephants, along with the lotus, adorning the entrances of many houses. Some of the finest murals of elephants playing in lotus pools may be seen in the rock-cut Buddhist monasteries at Ajanta and the ceilings of the Jaina temple in Sittanavasal. That such scenes also decorated ancient palaces is evident from Kalidasa's remarkably graphic and poignant description of the ancient palace of Rama which had already become derelict in his time. The walls of the palace, he writes, were once exquisitely painted with lotus-ponds in which huge elephants sported with their favorites and presented them with lotuses. The murals were so lifelike that wild animals who roamed amidst the ruins often mistook the images for real elephants and by jumping on them scratched the surfaces with their sharp claws. We can form some idea of such murals from several pictures illustrated here that show elephants sporting in water.

Some of the finest elephant images surviving from antiquity were rendered in terracotta. The impressive elephant from the third century B.C. may have been a votive object (29) and was perhaps offered to a village deity, as clay horses are today. Although not modeled quite as naturalistically as is usually the case in Indian art, the sculpture captures the majesty and strength of the animal with admirable accuracy. The Sri Lanka terracotta sculpture shows only the forepart of the elephant and probably served as a base for a Buddhist

shrine (29). In both India and Sri Lanka, elephants are often depicted in a row along the plinth of the temple, as if supporting the structure. Thus, apart from demonstrating the solidity of the buildings, they also symbolize the cosmic character of the shrine since elephants are symbols of the four directions. In contrast the two Indian sculptures display a sense of whimsy and playfulness. The small bust is a toy and is not unlike the clay toys that used to be available even in large cities forty years ago (31) but now have been replaced by far less imaginative and attractive plastic toys. A spoke would have passed through the hole and been attached to two wheels thus making a clay cart.

From a slightly later period we see a toy of a different kind (32). This time the animal is not only portrayed fully, but it also carries four riders. The curvature at the bottom and the hole for attaching rockers leave no doubt that it was meant to amuse a child. A much later toy, the bronze baby elephant from South India, is depicted in a posture that one rarely has the opportunity to observe in life (33). The representation is so alive as to remind us of a charming circus calf-elephant performing before its master.

Elephants with one or more riders remained a favorite motif with artists of South Asia. The beautiful example in ceramic, from Sawankhaloke in Thailand, may have been used as a candlestick (34). Another impressive candlestick, this time in bronze, is from Himachal Pradesh in India (35). The animal is rendered with an accuracy and simplicity quite unlike

48

33. *Calf Elephant*
    India, Tamilnadu, 13th century

34. *Elephant with Mahout*
    Thailand, Sawankhaloke, 14th–15th century

35. *Candlestick with Elephant and Riders*
    India, Chamba, 17th century

the self-conscious riders who sit so ceremoniously on the elephant's back. The driver of the elephant known as the mahout straddles the neck and carries an implement called an *ankusa* or elephant-goad.

As we admire the various representations of elephants in the art of South Asia, whether on tiles from Sri Lanka (36, 37), one of which retains its original paint, or a magnificent terracotta sculpture from Java (38), we are astonished by the great variety and novelty of the portrayals. In spite of stylized forms, the artists have always infused their subjects with the essential power of the animal. At the same time, however, by resorting to certain whimsical distortions, they have invariably made this ungainly creature friendly and lovable. If we compare the various representations from different regions, it becomes clear that elephants do indeed come in various shapes. This is also recognized by the many books that classify elephants according to shapes as well as characteristics and personalities. We may recall once again the Minai bowl from Iran in which a princely figure rides a spotted elephant (9). The elephant's spots may not necessarily be a figment of the artist's imagination for we are told by Valentijn that spotted elephants were especially admired in Sri Lanka and if one was found it was immediately taken to the king. It is possible that such a spotted elephant was sent by a king of Sri Lanka in the eleventh century to a Persian monarch and hence its appearance on the bowl. The dark figure

36. *Tile with Elephant*
Sri Lanka, 10th–12th century

37. *Tile with Elephant*
Sri Lanka, 10th–12th century

38. *Elephant*
Indonesia, East Java, 13th–14th century

50

riding behind the nimbate prince may well represent an Indian or Sinhalese elephant trainer.

The elephant has frequently been used as a decorative motif on the legs and backs of chairs and thrones. Many of the finest examples of such throne legs are made from ivory and will be discussed in chapter 4. On throne backs, the elephant is often shown supporting a lion or a mythical leonine animal (39). It would appear that the lion signifies sovereignty whereas the elephant symbolizes the four cardinal directions. Thus, the composite motif is perhaps a symbol of the cosmic power of the king or deity who sits upon the throne.

The penchant for more abstract animal shapes is illustrated by two delightful sculptures, one from Sri Lanka (40) and the other from Iran (41). It would be wrong for us to presume that the artists responsible for such lively representations were less than familiar with the animal's form. Rather, these small sculptures were perhaps intended simply for fun—hence their inventive and whimsical shapes. The charming Iranian elephant could well have served the same purpose as the equally attractive bronze representation from Sri Lanka. That some of the shapes were indeed meant to be both symbolic and amusing is clear from examples such as the marvelous elephant pots from Cambodia. The analogy between a pot and an elephant is obvious (42) and we have also seen that the animal often symbolizes water and rain. Perhaps such ceramic elephants in-

40. *Elephant*
Sri Lanka, date unknown

41. *Elephant*
Iran, 13th–14th century

fluenced the Thai or Cambodian sculptor to represent Indra's Airavata as he did in the temple relief (16). Once again such caricature-like distortions were intentional and do not reflect a lack of any technical skill on the part of the artist. On the contrary, the ceramic elephant (34) and the painting (19) from Thailand demonstrate clearly how competent the Thai artists were in depicting the animal.

By far the finest and most animated representations come from the artists of Mughal India in the sixteenth through eighteenth centuries. We have already referred to the great love the emperor Akbar had for his elephants and have on several occasions quoted Abul Fazal who has left us copious information on the subject. Apparently, Akbar had 101 elephants especially set aside for his own use. He was a great connoisseur and rider and, Abul Fazal's flattery notwithstanding, the following appraisal of imperial "elephantmanship" is impressive:

His majesty, the royal rider of the plain of auspiciousness, mounts on every kind of elephant, from the first to the last class, making them, notwithstanding their almost supernatural strength, obedient to his command. His majesty will put his foot on the tusk, and mount them even when they are in the rutting season, and astonishes experienced people.

Akbar's interest extended to the elephants of his courtiers as well, for we are told that "the elephants of the grandees are almost daily brought before His Majesty." One wonders how he

found time to take care of state business. Abul Fazal also gives detailed accounts of the huge bureaucracy that was set up to look after the imperial stables and, of course, the hunt. As a matter of fact, Akbar is said to have invented a new mode of hunting "which admits of remarkable *finesse*." In a Mughal picture (5) the emperor is seen hunting deer with great vigor and sagacity.

This digression about Akbar's keen interest in elephants will help explain their tremendous popularity in Indian paintings of this period. Although Akbar himself was only imitating the earlier native rulers in his almost deferential attitude, the Rajput princes who owed allegiance to the Mughal overlords were not far behind in their admiration for the animal. Each prince had his favorite elephants which were given fascinating personal names and whose likenesses were often perpetuated in pictures (45). Mughal and Rajput paintings abound in studies of elephants and it would not be an exaggeration to say that it was by far the most popular animal subject, and in Mughal pictures we find a new level of achievement that has rarely been surpassed both for accuracy and finesse.

Perhaps the most dramatic animal pictures of the Mughal period are those that show elephant fights (43). Obviously this was a favorite sport among the nobles; it was far more savage and bloody than a bullfight. We can do no better than quote the vivid eyewitness account of an elephant fight penned by

the French doctor and traveler, François Bernier, who visited India between 1566 and 1568.

> The festivals generally conclude with an amusement unknown in Europe—a combat between two elephants; which takes place in the presence of all the people on the sandy space near the river: the King, the principal ladies of the court, and the Omrahs viewing the spectacle from different apartments in the fortress.

A wall of earth is raised three or four feet wide and five or six high. Two ponderous beasts meet one another face to face, on opposite sides of the wall, each having a couple of riders, that the place of the man who sits on the shoulders, for the purpose of guiding the elephant with a large iron hook, may immediately be supplied if he should be thrown down. The

54

riders animate the elephants either by soothing words, or by chiding them as cowards, and urge them on with their heels, until the poor creatures approach the wall and are brought to the attack. The shock is tremendous, and it appears surprising that they survive the dreadful wounds and blows inflicted with their teeth, their heads, and their trunks. There are frequent pauses during the fight; it is suspended and renewed; and the mud wall being at length thrown down, the stronger or more courageous elephant passes on and attacks his opponent, and, putting him to flight, pursues and fastens upon him with so much obstinacy, that the animals can be separated only by means of cherkys, or fireworks, which are made to explode between them; for they are naturally timid, and have a particular dread of fire, which is the reason why elephants have been used with so very little advantage in armies since the use of fire-arms. The boldest come from Ceylon, but none are employed in war which have not been regularly trained, and accustomed for years to the discharge of muskets close to their heads, and the bursting of crackers between their legs.

This description seems to have been translated verbatim into two powerful drawings by eighteenth-century Rajput artists. In one, we see a fight in progress with the two elephants still separated by the mud wall, with groups of cheerleaders encouraging them (43), though not as gracefully as one sees in an American ball game. In the second picture, the two elephants have obviously brought down the wall and are now fighting tusk to tusk (44). In a third picture, though not connected with a fight, we see a corroboration of Bernier's observation that elephants must be tamed with fire and fireworks (45). Indeed, an inscription on the back of the picture tells us that the elephant's name was Chanchal, meaning "Rambunctious or Restless." We see several men using both torches and sparklers to tame Chanchal. Abul Fazal, too, tells us how elephants were trained this way to prepare them for the battlefield where they would encounter sounds of matchlocks and flashes of gunpowder. It was also customary to give them alcoholic drinks before the battle so that they would fight more ferociously.

One of the greatest of all elephant pictures is an eighteenth-century Indian miniature rendered by an unknown Bundi master (46). The artist has used great economy to create a picture that is both a strong visual metaphor and charming in its poetic evocation. We can feel the scorching heat of an Indian summer day as we look at the fiery red sky or the yellow ground. The rutting bull elephant in the center of the composition with his contorted shape and raised trunk reflects the unabashed sexual passion symbolized by the red and yellow. In the foreground a cow elephant cools off in a lotus pond, while two others seem to have gone mad with the heat as they wander about under the flaming sky, one trying to climb the rocks.

56

Apart from such delightful and imaginative representations of the animal, both the elephant hunt and the tusk have
been frequently used as symbols both in Mughal and Rajput
paintings. A type of painting that was very popular during this
period depicts visual images of musical modes (*raga* and
ragini). Each musical mode has an iconographic description
reflecting the appropriate emotional mood. One such mode is
known as *Kanhra* and its verbal and visual depictions are
closely associated with the elephant hunt. In a colorful rendering of this theme we see a captured elephant standing below a
pavilion (47). Above, a prince is seated within the pavilion, while
at the top of the stairway stands the god Krishna holding a
sword with his right hand and a tusk with the left. He is greeted
with a flywhisk by a panegyrist who sings the glories of the hunt.
The broken tusk here obviously symbolizes the horn of plenty.
Thus, although the picture represents a musical mode, its iconog-
raphy continues the ancient symbolism of regal splendor and
abundance associated with the elephant and the tusk.

Ganesa, The Elephant-Headed God

॥आनंदविलासरोपत्र॥॥प्रथमेकरना॥गणपतिनिहेंनमस्कारकदेहे॥नग बांना॥बहदंबऊस्यांयोंजेछा॥तिणीकरेसंसारकीधीर॥
साजेपरमानंदतिगांदेंनमस्कारकीधी॥

When to the wild dance of the trident-weaponed god
the hand of Nandin gladly beats the drum;
When then the drum draws by its sound of thunder
The Prince's peacock, out of fear of whom
swiftly the snake Sesa contracts his girth
and dives within the nostril of Ganesa's trunk,
Then does Ganesa trumpet loud and shake his head,
and may his nod for long be your protection,
which by the bees that fly up from his cheek sends music
to the four directions.
   Bhavabhuti (6th century) as translated by
   D.H.H. Ingalls

Ganesa, the elephant-headed god, is very special in Indian religions and mythology. The word *ganesa*, or *ganapti*, literally means "lord of the people or tribe." Ganas are the dwarf attendants of Siva and are often represented in art as diminutive, potbellied figures, some of whom have animal heads. Possibly the elephant-headed gana came to be chosen as the leader of the group and was known as Ganesa. Another possibility is that he is the adaptation of an ancient tribal totem. There are still tribes in India that have animals as totems, and since animals are very closely associated with almost all major deities in India, it seems reasonable to assume a direct derivation from tribal totems to attendants of the gods.

Exactly when Ganesa was adopted into the Hindu pantheon is uncertain but it probably happened before the birth of Christ. The elephant figures prominently among animals represented on seals of the Indus civilization, as already mentioned, and very likely all these animals had cultic significance. Worship of animals as well as of animal-headed deities is not confined to tribal cultures, but was widely practiced by the ancient civilizations of Egypt, Mesopotamia, and Persia. India is no exception, and it is natural that the elephant should have been venerated directly in early times. Ganesa was a pan-Indian god, like Sri-Lakshmi, the goddess of wealth and good fortune, and he is venerated alike by Hindus, Buddhists, and Jainas. Like Sri-Lakshmi, he is a household deity in India, Nepal, and Bali, the only other regions where Hinduism prevails today.

With Buddhism, Ganesa traveled to China, Korea, and Japan and he is revered in these countries as well. His cult was once strong in Afghanistan, as also in all countries of Southeast Asia where both Buddhism and Hinduism were transplanted from India in the early centuries of the Christian era. Some charming examples of Ganesa from Cambodia and Java are illustrated here.

Ganesa is universally popular as the god of auspiciousness and good fortune. It is very common for a Hindu, no matter what his or her sectarian persuasion, to preface all worship and all actions with the following invocation to Ganesa: I salute Ganapati (om ganapatayeh namah). He is the god who removes all obstacles and hence is invoked and venerated by all merchants at the start of a new year. No action, in fact, is undertaken by a Hindu without invoking Ganesa, and in the frontispiece of an illuminated text, which has nothing to do with Ganesa, we see the god being worshiped (48). The biggest annual festival of Ganesa is celebrated with great pomp and ceremony, particularly by the merchant communities of Bombay and other cities. Despite their veneration of Ganesa, however, Buddhists sometimes characterized the "obstacle-remover" as the very symbol of "obstacles" and invented images that display this sectarian hostility. In such depictions a Buddhist deity is seen trampling upon a prostrate figure of Ganesa.

A number of different myths have been invented to explain Ganesa's birth (49). At times he is considered to be Siva's son, created without the help of his spouse, Parvati; at others, Parvati alone creates the infant. Although all the myths are both charming and imaginative, we will confine ourselves to only three versions.

Disturbed by the unruly conduct of Siva's barbarous dwarf attendants at the Saiva temple of Somnath, the gods appealed to Siva himself to find some means of subduing them. On hearing their appeal Siva began to meditate. As he did so, a brilliant light emanated from his forehead and assumed the shape of a wondrous infant. His wife, however, was distressed that Siva should have created a child without her and uttered the following curse: "May thy head resemble that of an elephant and thy body be deformed by a huge belly." Siva counterbalanced the curse by ordaining that his son would be known as Ganesa and must always be invoked and venerated before the other gods on all occasions. If not, any worship would invariably be futile.

In the second version of the Ganesa myth, Siva was reluctant to take any action against his followers and so sent the gods to his wife, Parvati. On hearing their complaints, Parvati gently rubbed her body and, from the divine dirt and unguents, produced a child who was named "the Remover of Obstacles."

Far richer is the myth where both Siva and Parvati participate in Ganesa's creation (50). Although married for many years, they had remained childless which saddened Parvati. When she discussed the matter with her husband, she found that Siva preferred his carefree life and was not enthusiastic about raising a family. To console her, however, he took a piece of her garment and made a doll for her to play with. Although dissatisfied, Parvati pretended to feed the rag doll and miraculously it came to life. Overjoyed, Parvati handed the infant to Siva who laid it down and realized that under the influence of the evil planet, Saturn, the boy would be short-lived. A few minutes later, the infant's head fell off.

Seeing Parvati distraught at the loss of her son, Siva decided to put the head back, but he was unsuccessful. A voice from the skies told him that the head would not fit, and that he must find a creature whose head faced north and graft it on to the infant. Siva then dispatched his bull Nandin, who arrived at Indra's kingdom and found the divine elephant Airavata facing north. After a great fight with Indra, Nandin managed to cut off the elephant's head which was then placed on Ganesa's shoulders. While Parvati was ecstatic, Siva had to console Indra who had just lost his mount. Siva then told Indra to throw the elephant's headless body into the celestial ocean, where it would grow a new head and reappear during the churning of the ocean. A variant of the story of Airavata's emergence from the sea is told on page 28.

Ganesa is usually depicted as a potbellied dwarf with four

63

arms. He generally carries a battle-axe, a weapon that destroys both obstacles and ignorance, or an elephant-goad. Among his other attributes are a noose, a rosary, a radish, a bunch of mangoes, a broken tusk or a pen, and a bowl of sweets. The radish, the bunch of mangoes, the tusk, and the rat probably have fertility symbolism; the rosary is emblematic of his ascetic nature, for, like his father, he too is a yogi. The bowl of sweets possibly symbolizes abundance as well as his childishness, and in a charming representation from Nepal we see his spouse actually feeding him. Even though an adolescent god, he does have a wife whose name, Pushti, means prosperity, again emphasizing Ganesa's role as a deity of abundance and fertility (51).

Incongruous as it seems, the rat or mouse is usually Ganesa's mount, (52) probably because of this animal's uncanny ability to gnaw through every obstacle in order to reach its goal. As Zimmer has very aptly stated:

As the rat makes his way through all obstacles into the security of the granary, there to consume the rice stores of the village household, and as the elephant in the jungle forges mightily ahead, trampling and uprooting vegetation standing in its way, so Ganesa, "The Lord of Obstacles" *(vighnaisvara),* breaks a path for the devotee.

Sometimes, however, Ganesa rides a lion which is generally his mother's mount.

Although he may have more than four arms and five

65

52. *Ganesa Seated on His Rat*
India, Himachal Pradesh, 12th century

53. *Dancing Ganesa*
Nepal, 12th century

54. *Ganesa*
Indonesia, East Java, 15th century

66

heads, Ganesa always has a single tusk which is why he is called Ekadanta or One-tusked. One myth tells us that the tusk was lost by Airavata while Nandin was trying to cut off Airavata's head to graft it on the headless Ganesa. The explanation seems contrived, however, in view of the fact that Ganesa often carries his broken tusk. Thus, the tusk may well be a horn of plenty. Far more charming is the following story which also tells of his inordinate passion for sweets which, too, is a symbol of abundance.

One night after a grand feast, at which he stuffed himself with sweets, as good brahmins still do, Ganesa returned home riding his rat. Unable to bear the additional weight, the rat dropped him and the sight was so funny that the moon in the sky began to laugh. This upset Ganesa very much, and, not having anything else handy, he broke off one of his tusks and hurled it at the moon. This is why the moon has all those marks on its face.

While the mythographers were busy inventing charming myths to explain the origins and symbology of the god, the poets were concerned with his divine personality and his adolescent behavior. Like his father Ganesa loves to dance, and Rajasekhara (11th century) has written a beautiful poem describing his dance, which vividly captures the spirit and expressiveness of the lively representations of the dancing god (51, 53).

May the dancing god Ganesa be your aid,
copied by the guardian elephants of the horizon,
who spring up lightly from the earth that trembles
at the stamping of his feet,
The while with upraised trunk he drinks and then
sprays back
like drops of water the great circle of the stars.

We have mentioned that sometimes Ganesa carries a pen, and when he does he is regarded as the divine scribe. We are told that when Vyasa, the author of the enormous epic *Mahabharata*, could not find a mortal stenographer who could take his dictation fast enough, Ganesa volunteered and wrote the massive epic faster than Vyasa could dictate. Ganesa's wisdom is demonstrated in a charming verse ascribed to the poet Mandana. Puzzled by the androgynous form of their parents, Ganesa's youngest brother, Kartikeya, asked:

"When father and when mother became a single
body, what happened, elder brother, to the
other halves of each other?"
Victory to Ganesa, who explains to the young
prince, "The one on earth was born as everyman,
the other every woman."

In many other beautiful and humorous poems, the poets have exploited the relationship between the two brothers with great perception and psychological insight.

55. *Ganesa*
Indonesia, Central Java, 9th–10th century

56. *Ganesa*
India, Himachal Pradesh, 16th century

57. *Ganesa*
Cambodia, 12th century

58. *Ganesa*
Cambodia, 12th century

59. *Embracing Elephant-headed Deities (Kangi-ten)*
Japan, 15th century

One of the nicest is the charming story in Bengali: One day Ganesa and Kartikeya were arguing in front of their mother as to who could go around the world faster. Kartikeya immediately flew off on his peacock. Ganesa, however, simply circled his mother and stood victorious.

It would be impossible to illustrate the wide variety of Ganesa images that occur in the arts of South Asia. No matter how modest the representation, it is always informed with a sense of whimsy, bordering almost on caricature. Artists obviously have taken great delight in fashioning likenesses which are both inventive and charming (54, 55). Often there is a noticeable contrast between a spontaneously rendered "folk" piece, such as a small chalkstone piece from Java, and a more dignified and sophisticated bronze. Another popular piece, this time from India, is carved in wood and reflects a most attractive fusion of abstract shapes with amusing expressiveness (56). Some of the most delightful representations of Ganesa are encountered in Cambodian bronzes. In one we see him almost as an embarrassed child, standing with a tusk in his right hand and the left hand supporting his trunk (57). In another he sits like an obese and prosperous shopkeeper, smug and secure in his affluence (58).

The most curious representation of Ganesa may be seen in certain Japanese images called Kangi-ten, in which two elephant-headed figures embrace each other like long lost

friends (59). In the ninth century the cult of Kangi-ten was introduced into Japan from China by the famous Buddhist monk Kobo Daishi. According to the Shingon sect of Buddhism, the divine couple symbolizes the union of the Soul of the Universe with the Primordial Essence. The images are always made of metal and were seen only by the initiated. Although the two figures represent a male and a female, the sexual differences are hardly apparent.

Some of the finest portrayals occur in late Indian paintings, where the god's elephant head does not seem to detract in any way from the natural charm and wit reflected in the pictures. In a nineteenth-century representation, four-armed Ganesa lies as naturally in his mother's lap as would a normal baby (60). The entire family is depicted in another beautiful picture, painted about 1800 (61). The hide of the elephant Gajasura, de-

stroyed by Siva, serves as a rug. Kartikeya occupies his mother's lap, while Siva strokes the young Ganesa to sleep. Although the personages are divine, the scene vividly depicts a somewhat tired family relaxing in the warm sun on a winter day.

In this painting, lying beside his father, Ganesa looks very much like a "teddy bear." In a sense, Ganesa is the Indian teddy bear as well as a security blanket: he is loved by everyone and rubbing his belly is said to bring good luck. In the Indian sculpture gallery of the Los Angeles County Museum of Art there is a fine stone image of Ganesa with an enormous belly. When it was first displayed a decade ago, the image was white. Now the belly is black, because countless visitors have rubbed it, and still do, even though they are unaware of the Indian belief. Like a teddy bear or a favorite pet, Ganesa simply invites the loving touch.

60. *Parvati Nursing Ganesa*
North India, 19th century

61. *The Holy Family*
India, Rajput Style, Mandi School, c. 1800

70

Ivories

Notwithstanding the elephant's great usefulness to man, the animal has been a tragic victim of our greed. Since antiquity their tusks have been in great demand, principally to create products that have catered to man's vanity rather than his needs. Ivory has been used extensively for jewelery, cosmetic articles, furnishings, such as caskets and boxes, beds, chairs, palanquins, and thrones. Doors, pillars, and even entire pavilions in ancient palaces and parkways were frequently made of ivory. In ancient texts such as the Indian epic *Ramayana* we read of walls and pillars being inlaid with ivory and of princes riding in chariots that were beautifully embellished with ivory. The *Mahavamsa* of Sri Lanka informs us that king Parakrama Bahu (1164–1197) made a park railed "with pillars decorated with rows of images made of ivory." One can appreciate the desire to use the smooth, satin-white material to enrich surfaces of objects, but as so often the products were painted, it is difficult to understand why something less expensive than ivory was not used.

Although as raw material African ivory is considered superior to the South Asian specimen, we know that Indian ivory products have been in considerable demand since ancient times. An inscription on the palace of Darius I (c. 522–486 B.C.) at Susa in Iran informs us that ivory was brought from Sind, now part of Pakistan. One of the finest ivory statuettes carved in India was recovered from the ruins of Pompeii, destroyed in A.D. 79; the statuette is now preserved in the museum at Naples. A graphic example of Indians bearing ivories occurs in the well-known "Barberini Diptych" now in the Louvre in Paris (62). The diptych is said to have been carved about A.D. 540 and represents a triumphant Justinian. Along the bottom two Indians wearing dhotis and turbans bring an elephant, a tusk, and a tiger, presumably gifts sent to the emperor. Not only were tusks and ivories exported but it appears that even ivory-carvers traveled outside the country. An ancient Buddhist text has preserved an amusing story about such a carver who was considered a master of realism, superior even to Greek sculptors. The carver is said to have visited a Greek city, possibly Alexandria, where he called on a colleague. As an orthodox Indian, the carver carried his rice with him and gave it to the lady of the house, asking her to cook it. Returning several hours later, he found an embarrassed lady sitting with a pot of uncooked rice. The grains were made from ivory! It may be pointed out that dishonest Indian grain traders still play this trick upon consumers, but today the chips that are mixed with rice are made from stone rather than ivory.

In both India and Sri Lanka ivory-carvers were all-round craftsmen and enjoyed a high rank in the hierarchy of artists. An inscription on one of the much admired gateways of the great Buddhist monument at Sanchi (100 B.C.–A.D. 100) informs us that the reliefs were donated and executed by the ivory-carvers of the city of Vidisa. The carving process is similar to that used for wood and stone and virtually the same tools are employed. The process may be described briefly as follows. The finest ivory for carving is that which has been freshly sawed off a live animal. First boiled in a solution of water mixed with soda and calcium to make it soft for easy cutting, the large pieces of ivory are then sawed into smaller sections, always in the direction of the grain to prevent fracture. Then the heavy outer bark is removed and the sections are sawed further to the required size. An outline of the image is drawn on the surface with charcoal or pencil and the ivory fixed in a vise. The desired shape is then carved out with a small chisel and a wooden mallet. This is, of course, the hardest part of the work and requires great skill and diligence because of the delicacy of the ivory.

After the roughly cut form has been smoothed with a file, the object is polished to give it the attractive satinlike finish that elicits our admiration. Several methods of polishing ivory are known in South Asia. An ancient method, now abandoned, was to rub the piece with the powder of the dried tongue of a fish, called "kanana," applied with a wet cloth. A second method is to use the central rib of the leaf of the breadfruit tree. Dipped in water, the rib's rough surface when rubbed on the ivory provides an attractive shine. But the most common means is to polish with ivory dust itself. As already mentioned, the objects sometimes were painted in polychrome, as is the comb from

63. *Comb with Dancing Female*
Sri Lanka, 18th century

South India (63) or the Buddha image from Sri Lanka (97).

The objects discussed here are from a wide geographical region and a long span of time. While the majority of objects are from India, there are several from Nepal, Tibet, Burma, Bali, and Sri Lanka. The destructive tropical climate of South Asia is not very conducive to the prolonged survival of ivory objects, and utilitarian items such as combs, ornaments, or furnishings wore out easily. Sanskrit literature, both religious and secular, is nevertheless rich in allusions to the use of ivory, and archaeological excavations at the Indus Valley civilization sites have yielded a surprising quantity of ivory objects. Within the subcontinent, ivory appears to have been more popular in certain regions than in others. One of the great emporia of India, mentioned by the classical geographer Ptolemy, was situated in Orissa and was called Dantapura or city of the tusk. It was from this port that Buddhist monks set sail in the fourth century B.C. to carry the new religion to Sri Lanka. The tradition of ivory-carving is still alive in the coastal state of Orissa and in the southern states of Karnataka, Tamilnadu, and Kerala.

SECULAR OBJECTS

Much jewelry was made from ivory as is evident not only from ancient Indian literature but also from the writings of foreigners. In his *Indika*, Arrian records how Indians loved to wear ear ornaments made of ivory. Some of these adornments

may be seen represented in sculpture but very few actual ear-
rings have survived. Tribal peoples in many parts of India, especially in Assam, still wear jewelery made from ivory. In previous
centuries one of the most popular objects of ivory was the
comb. Accustomed as we are today to grooming our hair with
plain, plastic combs, it may be difficult to imagine that once
people devoted much greater attention to this apparently
modest implement of vanity. Not only were combs and hair
pins made from ivory and horn, but often they were beautifully
decorated.

Although the two combs from Sri Lanka illustrated
here (63, 64) are of relatively recent origin, they continue earlier
shapes and decoration. Retaining much of its polychromy, one
of the combs is embellished with identical motifs on both sides.
Two fly whisk-bearing females stand and watch a female
dancer who carries a sword and a shield. The principal motif
on the other comb is a pair of birds, and in both, the central
sections are enriched with stylized floral designs and geometric
patterns. Most combs from Sri Lanka are decorated in a similar
manner.

The much rarer comb from Nepal, in the Himalayas, is
embellished with a religious image, the Hindu god Vishnu
seated on a lotus and surrounded by a circle of light (65). As we
will see with other objects of daily use, it was not unusual to
decorate ostensibly secular articles with religious imagery. Ob-

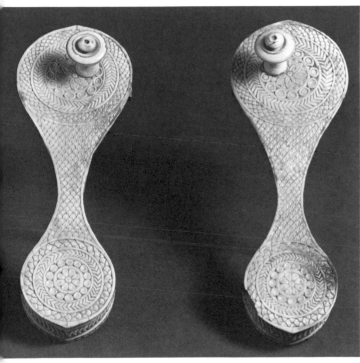

...iously the owner of this comb was a devout Vaishnava. Possibly both the Nepalese comb and the one topped with a heraldic lion (66) served as hairpins. The pin with the lion is also decorated with a frieze of dancing figures which are remarkably lively and well executed.

A rather unusual use of ivory may be seen in a pair of eighteenth-century sandals (67). Such sandals were used in India, particularly by the brahmins and religious preceptors, or gurus,

77

who considered shoes made from animal hide unclean. In this remarkably well-preserved pair the visible surface has been richly carved with geometric and vegetative patterns. Since ivory is a cool and smooth material, such sandals are quite comfortable and certainly more elegant than wooden sandals which were the more common footwear for the less affluent.

Ivory was used extensively and in many different ways for boxes, caskets, and furniture. Some items were made entirely of ivory; others were decorated with ivory panels that covered the whole surface; and still others were richly inlaid with ivory. Generally, the design was carved, but occasionally it was lightly etched. There are also fine examples of openwork rendered with great skill and delicacy.

In most boxes and chests we encounter the artist's great delight for sinuous and rhythmic plant motifs, a penchant that is deeply rooted in ancient tradition. Whether the object is a small cylindrical container from Sri Lanka (68) or an impressive chest from Mughal India (69), the surfaces are invariably filled with exuberant plant and floral motifs (70). The two large chests of drawers were made in Mughal India and exhibit two different techniques of workmanship. One of them is decorated with beautiful panels filled with lush vegetation. The gracefully

78

79

undulating stems and flowers are carved with extraordinary finesse. The second Mughal chest of drawers is inlaid with ivory, and here we encounter a greater variety of subjects than can be illustrated here. The panel we have chosen shows the strong influence of contemporary Iranian styles and motifs. The reclining youth, the split palmette, the *sidra* or tree of life, and the lion triumphing over the antelope are all familiar in Iranian art. The Mughals were ardent admirers of Iranian culture and hence one often encounters Iranian themes and motifs in Indian art of this period.

Boxes or chests such as these must have yielded the isolated plaques that provide us with tantalizing glimpses of life in a court or a noble mansion. Two slender panels from the seventeenth century show various figures, probably members of the nobility, seated in cartouches and holding nosegays or parrots (71, 72). Tigers and antelopes alternate along the base, while the remaining space is filled with botanic motifs. Elegant as these figures are, two fine plaques from Orissa are even more attractive. In one we see a turbaned and bearded man accompanied by an ascetic dwarf or attendant (73); in the other a lady is playing with a ball (74). With his outstretched arm, the man, who may represent a royal personage, appears to be offering a flower, perhaps to a deity. The lady amusing herself with a ball is indeed a charming depiction of a subject that has remained extremely popular with Indian artists and poets.

82

Erotic themes decorating headpieces of royal beds or chairs were especially popular in Orissa. All of them portray couples engaged in love-making and some are far more explicit than the two illustrated here (75, 76). Although one is from about A.D. 1300 and the other from the early seventeenth century, we notice that four hundred years have produced very little change in either the design or the composition. Invariably the lovers are seen within an arched pavilion and the figures are completely cut away and modeled in the round. The quality of carving is much finer in the earlier piece, while the later example is more ornately decorated.

Among other items of furniture, a large number of throne or chair legs have survived, mostly from Orissa (77). They represent some of the most dynamic renderings ever created of animals in ivory—especially of the elephant and lion—and the carving is often extremely elaborate and detailed. Both animals are frequently shown in rearing positions (78). The rearing lion, alone or triumphing over an elephant, is an ancient motif in Indian art. Sometimes the elephant and the lion are combined into one hybrid creature with the body of a lion and the head and trunk of an elephant (79). It would appear that the combined strength of these two animals was a symbol of the invincible power of the king, who is frequently compared to them in literature; the motif is often seen on thrones of divine images as well as those of mortal kings.

Of unusual quality and rarity are four corner pieces which probably decorated a flat seat of some kind. The elephant here is on its knees, completely humbled by the enormous snarling lion (80). By distorting their proportions, the sculptor leaves no doubt about which animal is the stronger of the two. On either side is a pair of putto-like figures who appear to be doing some acrobatic riding. With one foot placed on the foreleg of the lion and the other bent in the flying posture, they seem to be balancing themselves like expert riders as they hold the reins emerging from the lion's mouth. The winged figures probably represent angels and are rendered with astonishing naturalism. In contrast, the head of the lion is stylized and conveys a sense of enormous strength.

For bold imagination and technical dexterity, the Orissan throne legs remain unexcelled (79, 81). In earlier examples the lions and elephants were represented more or less naturalistically, while those of the sixteenth and seventeenth centuries reveal a more complex vision with contorted bodies and impossible postures. Creatures of fantasy whose strength is no longer menacing, they reflect the artist's almost mystical delight in making his forms enigmatic though enticing. One is also kept guessing as to which is the front and which the rear, for tails are provided on both sides and sometimes even emerge from lotuses. The subject is further enriched by a solitary female on one side standing like a dancer about to perform, while on the

84

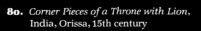

80. *Corner Pieces of a Throne with Lion,*
India, Orissa, 15th century

81. *Throne Leg with Rearing Lion Motif*
India, Orissa, 17th century

other side two or more warriors are riding their horses. More-over, almost the entire surface is richly adorned with a luxuriant lion's mane, lush foliage, and bands of delicately carved ornaments that make the leg as sumptuous as an Indian feast.

The dexterity of the ivory-carver is particularly clear in the delicately carved throne backs which were often cut through to create a silhouette-like design. In both complexity and inventiveness, these openwork panels remain the tour de force of ivory carving. Frequently the animals depicted are composite creatures as in an eighteenth-century panel (82). On the right, a

male archer confronts the female archer on the left. Their fantastic horse and elephant mounts are composed of female musicians. If we are to believe the seventeenth-century French traveler, Tavernier, these representations depict the weird whims of the princes, for he writes:

These women have so much suppleness that when the king wishes to visit . . . , nine of them very cleverly represented the form of an elephant, four making the four feet, four others the body and one the trunk, and the king mounted above . . . in that way made his entry into the town.

83. *Dagger with a Ram Handle*
India, 17th century

84. *Sword* (kris) *with Demoness*
Indonesia, Bali, 19th century

The same "sport," if we may call it that, apparently appealed to the Thais as well for there, too, we find paintings that portray elephants composed of women and angels.

Since ancient times ivory has remained a popular material for the handles of swords, daggers, and canes, and during the Mughal period for gunpowder horns as well. The handle of a small knife (83), perhaps used by a noble lady to peel fruit, is a beautifully carved ram's head that shows the careful naturalism for which the Mughal animal studies are justly admired. The simple elegance of this Mughal knife handle may be contrasted with the elaborately carved handle of a Balinese sword, or *kris* (84). The demon here was no doubt meant to frighten the enemy as well as to strengthen the arm of the swordsman.

Ivory gunpowder horns from seventeenth-century Mughal India are among the finest objects carved in this material. The example illustrated here is a tour de force and reveals an unknown master's extraordinary use of animal forms to enhance the beauty of an essentially utilitarian object (85). Not only are the animals cleverly integrated into the form of the object itself, but their own shapes and activity infuse the horn with a life of its

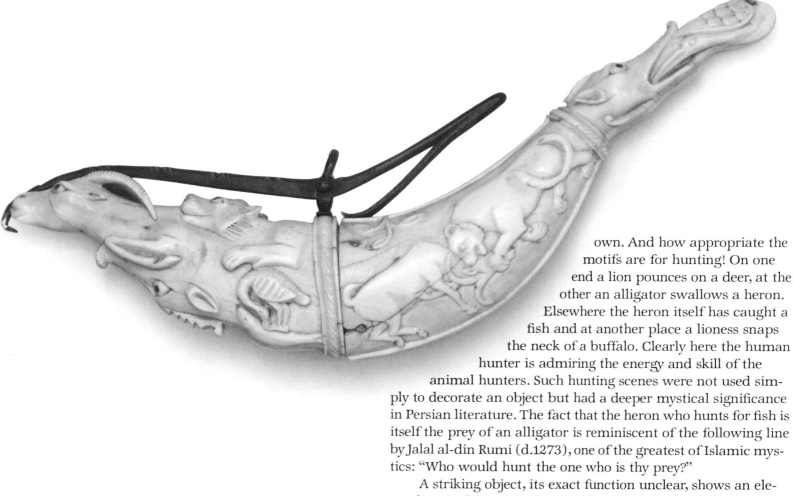

own. And how appropriate the motifs are for hunting! On one end a lion pounces on a deer, at the other an alligator swallows a heron. Elsewhere the heron itself has caught a fish and at another place a lioness snaps the neck of a buffalo. Clearly here the human hunter is admiring the energy and skill of the animal hunters. Such hunting scenes were not used simply to decorate an object but had a deeper mystical significance in Persian literature. The fact that the heron who hunts for fish is itself the prey of an alligator is reminiscent of the following line by Jalal al-din Rumi (d.1273), one of the greatest of Islamic mystics: "Who would hunt the one who is thy prey?"

A striking object, its exact function unclear, shows an elegantly attired female archer standing on a cylindrical base (86). The cylinder is carved with other figures of women, either walking or riding horses, obviously hunting companions of the archer. There is little doubt that she is a princess of the Mughal period, for during that era scenes of ladies hunting became a popular type of painting. Such ivories were closely related to the art of painting, as is evident from another example of which only the base has survived (87). The scene represented around this base portrays the *ragini* Kakubha, which is a musical mode. In this mode a peacock dances while the heroine plays a vina. Both

89

88. *Portrait of an Englishman*
India, c. 1800

89. *Portrait of an Indian*
India, c. 1800

ivories are from the Deccan, very likely the old Hyderabad state.

Ivory objects remained in great demand during the British period in both India and Sri Lanka, and chess sets as well as various other objects depicting the people and fauna of the region were taken back to Europe as souvenirs. As often happens, artists now began to produce objects whose function was purely decorative. European influence is clearly discernible in the pair of carvings portraying two gentlemen, one English and the other Indian (88, 89). More impressive for its simplicity and hieratic majesty is a portrait of a nobleman from Kandy in Sri Lanka (90). It is obvious that the unknown artist understood his medium well.

RELIGIOUS OBJECTS

The use of ivory for creating religious images was more popular with the Buddhists than with the Hindus or Jainas. In keeping with their insistence on non-violence, the Jainas did not approve of the use of ivory since removing the tusks meant hurting the animal. Hindus, however, may have had different reasons. Ivory and all other bones are generally regarded as unclean and hence unsuitable for fashioning divine images. This is one reason why so few ivory portrayals of Hindu deities exist today. The attractive carving of the boy Krishna playing the flute was made in the early part of this century, probably as a decorative object rather than an image to be worshiped (91). Similarly, the

lovely South Indian plaque portraying Yasoda swinging the baby Krishna must have had an edifying purpose and possibly was meant to decorate a throne (92). Even if the Hindus did not make images of their gods in ivory, they did use the material for thrones and other sacred objects. Many of the chair legs we have already discussed may have once supported thrones of deities. The charming Nepalese panel decorated on both sides with images of Vishnu and exquisitely carved serpents must have served as a throne back (93). Horns of plenty, often made from ivory or bone, were dedicated to deities of abundance, and even now in many parts of India, especially in the hills, we can see horns of animals decorating the facade of a temple. In Tantric Hinduism implements of bone as well as skulls of both animals and humans play an important role.

Yet, the majority of ivory objects that have survived are Buddhist, and some of the finest were rendered in eighth-century Kashmir. As examples of ivory sculpture they remain unsurpassed and attest to the extraordinary skill and imagination of Kashmiri ivory-carvers. A charming fragment, now consisting of six deeply carved figures, must once have formed part of a more elaborate tableau in which the Buddha, Sakyamuni, is sur-

93

94

rounded by gods and ascetics (94). Four of the six figures in the fragment appear to be adoring the Buddha, who would have sat in the middle of the relief. The figure above blows a trumpet, while the figure at the bottom is obviously a demon. It is very likely that the fragment belonged to a relief representing the occasion when the Buddha was attacked by the hordes of Mara, the Buddhist god of desire, in an attempt to distract the Master from gaining enlightenment. The incident is conceptually similar to Satan's temptation of Christ in the New Testament. The carving seems even more accomplished in the fragment than in the more complete tableau of Buddha visited by Indra (95), although there seems little doubt that both were produced in the same atelier. The undercutting is even deeper and the figures are carved completely in the round.

In a rare religious object from seventeenth-century Burma, the artist has taken a large portion of a tusk and filled the surface with many images of the Buddha (96). All the figures are represented in identical fashion: each Buddha is seated in the lotus posture with his left hand placed on his lap and the right touching the earth. The gesture symbolizes the Buddha's enlightenment at Bodhgaya.

Images of the Buddha were also carved from ivory in Sri Lanka, especially at Kandy. Although the two illustrated here were once painted, only the fine standing image retains some polychromy (97, 98). Buddhist monks generally wear both

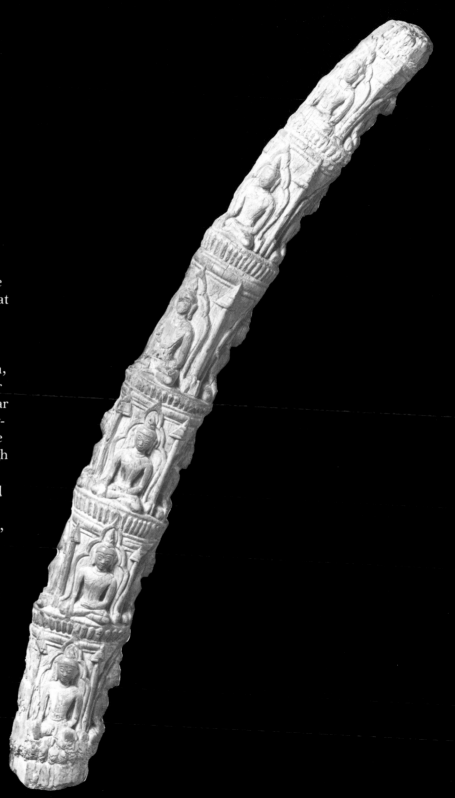

red and yellow garments. Typical of the Kandy style, the garments are indicated by wavy linear striations that create a rippling surface which imparts a sense of motion to these otherwise static though statuesque figures.

Although not many ivories from Tibet are known, bone of all kinds has been a popular medium in Tibetan religious art. In fact, many religious articles can only be made of bone that is said to possess magical qualities. Several Tibetan ivory sculptures are illustrated here and all are of superb quality. Carved in the round, the fourteenth-century pair of Bodhisattvas may once have flanked a Buddha image; the pair is Sino-Tibetan in style (99). Both were once richly polychromed and the remaining colors provide an interesting surface.

Of the same style is a remarkable sculpture representing a creature known as *Daka* in Sanskrit and *Za-byed* in Tibetan. His Sanskrit name signifies one who "calls," while the Tibetan expression means the "devourer" (100). When rendered in metal, the figure serves as an incense-burner, but this superb ivory could not be for that purpose. One of the finest Sino-Tibetan ivory objects, the figure is carved with consummate skill. Slight traces of color indicate his tiger skin and the details are rendered with great finesse.

Less dramatic but equally well-carved is the Tibetan ivory representing the mystic-saint Padmasambhava (101). Known as Guru Rimpoche in Tibet, he went there from India in the eighth

97

98

102. *Phur-bu (Ritual Dagger)*
Tibet, 17th century

104. *Fan*
Sri Lanka, Kandy, 18th century

103. *Stupa*
Sri Lanka, Kandy, 18th century

century and has remained the most exalted teacher of Buddhism in that country. Although he was an historical figure, his image is idealized. Always represented as a heavily clothed monk, he holds a thunderbolt and a skullcup, two of the most important ritual implements of esoteric Buddhism. Noteworthy is the artist's skillful rendering of the multiple folds of the garments and the frowning, expressive face.

Ivory was also used extensively to make Buddhist ritual objects. A fine example is a *phur-bu*, or magic dagger, used by Tibetan priests to exorcise evil spirits (102). The blade of the dagger has three faces and ends in a point sharp enough to pierce an enemy's heart. The handle is carved into heads of terrifying deities, facing the four cardinal directions. The cosmic forces, therefore, are gathered from all sides and channeled to the point of the dagger. The beautifully proportioned stupa and fan are from Sri Lanka (103, 104). The stupa is one of the most important symbols of Buddhism, while the fan is used ceremonially during processions. Both are handsomely decorated with geometric and floral designs that are either incised or painted, and the clasps of the handle

101

that hold the fan are richly carved with stylized floral scrolls.

Apart from the Hindus and Buddhists, the Christians in South Asia too have used ivory extensively for religious imagery (105). Some of the finest Christian ivories were produced in the former Portuguese colony of Goa in India. Situated north of Bombay on the west coast, Goa and its surrounding regions were occupied by the Portuguese in the sixteenth century. After that time Goa became a bastion of the Catholic religion in India and was closely associated with St. Xavier. Until recently, the saint's body, miraculously preserved for over three centuries, was on public view there. It was from Goa that priests of the Jesuit order went to Agra and attended the Mughal court. Ivory was a popular medium with the Christians in Europe from the Byzantine age onward, and we have already discussed the famous "Barberini Diptych" (62). It was natural, therefore, for the Christians of Goa to make images in ivory—mostly for domestic use. No new motif entered the ivory-carver's repertory, and Goanese pieces usually portray the crucified Christ, the Madonna and Child, or saints of the Church in conventional forms (106–108). Inevitably, though, the sculptures reflect an Indian feeling which is more readily experienced than described. The sculpture of St. John (108) best expresses this "Indianness," for the Indians have always loved to depict infants and children in art. Except for his European attire, St. John is as sweet and loving a figure as any boy Krishna (91). In terms of style the figures have nothing new to offer and they continue Portuguese Baroque mannerisms. Some of the representations, however, such as the Madonna and Child enthroned, reflect much earlier modes. Obviously the Goanese artists had a variety of European models at their disposal which they continued to copy into the twentieth century.

103

Bibliographical Notes

Many of the English verses quoted in the Introduction are from the most useful and entertaining book, *Elephants Ancient and Modern* (New York: The Viking Press, 1968) by F. C. Sillar and R. M. Meyler. Another general book on the subject with beautiful illustrations is L. P. Winfrey's *The Unforgettable Elephant* (New York: Walker and Company, 1980). For Lord Kenneth Clark's views on prehistoric animal drawings see *Animals and Men* (New York: William Morrow and Company, Inc., 1977). A scholarly book on the subject of elephants in the classical world is H. H. Scullard's *The Elephant in the Greek and Roman World* (Ithaca: Cornell University Press, 1974). As a matter of fact, the book is a rich source for the study of the Indian elephant as well. For the elephant in Indian art see S. V. Gorakshakar's *Animals in Indian Art* (Bombay: Prince of Wales Museum, 1979).

Quotations about the elephant in Vedic literature are from R. Panikkar's *The Vedic Experience* (Berkeley, Los Angeles, and London: University of California Press, 1977). The verses from the Tamil *Kuruntokai* and the *Panchatantra* material are from *An Anthology of Indian Literature*, edited by J. B. Alphonso-Karkala (Pelican paperback: 1971). For the *Mahabharata*, I have used J. A. B. Van Buitnen's translation published by the University of Chicago Press. The references to Kalidasa's *Meghaduta* are from L. Nathan, *The Transport of Love* (Berkeley, Los Angeles, London: University of California Press, 1976). Abul Fazal's *Ain-i-Akbari* is a rich source for elephant lore during the Mughal period and the translation I have used is by H. Blochman and published by the Asiatic Society in Calcutta in 1939.

There are many books by foreigners who visited India, most of which contain interesting references to the elephant and ivory. Apart from Scullard's book mentioned above, the three that I have used extensively are: J. W. McCrindle, *Ancient India as Described by Megasthenes and Arrian* (Calcutta: Chuckervertty, Chatterjee and Co., Ltd., 1960); F. Bernier, *Travels in the Moghul Empire* (New Delhi: S. Chand and Co. (Pvt) Ltd., 2nd ed. 1972); and S. Arasaratnam, ed. and tr.: *François Valentijn's Description of Ceylon* (London: The Hakluyt Society, 1978).

For the Jataka tales concerning the elephant see H. T. Francis and E. J. Thomas, *Jataka Tales* (Bombay: Jaico Publishing House, 1957). H. Zimmer's *Myths and Symbols in Indian Art*, published in the Bollingen Series and easily available in paperback, is a good introduction to many of the mythological stories about the elephant. For Ganesa, the best available book still is Alice Getty's *Ganeśa*, (Oxford: The Clarendon Press, 1936), reprinted in an Indian edition. For Indian ivories the most comprehensive survey, with an extensive bibliography, is V. P. Dwivedi's *Indian Ivories* (Delhi: Agam Prakashan, 1976). A. K. Coomaraswamy's *Mediaeval Sinhalese Art* (New York: Pantheon Books, 2nd ed. 1956) has a useful discussion about the craft of ivory-carving in twentieth-century Sri Lanka. Generally, however, very little has been written about either the elephant or ivory in Sri Lanka or Southeast Asia. Some fine pictures of elephants in Thai art are illustrated in J. Boisselier's *Thai Painting* (Tokyo, New York, and San Francisco: Kodansha International, 1976) which I have used with much profit.

List of Illustrations

An asterisk denotes an object not in the exhibition. Unless otherwise indicated all objects belong to the Los Angeles County Museum of Art.

1. *Animals Including the Elephant*
France, Antonio Lafreri (1512–1580)
Engraving; 12½ x 17½ in.
(31.6 x 44.4 cm.)
Gift of Irene Salinger in memory of her father, Adolph Stern
54.70.10

2. *Elephant*
India, Rajput Style, Kotah School,
18th century
Ink on paper; 10¼ x 11⅞ in.
(26.0 x 30.3 cm.)
Mrs. Leroy Davidson Collection

3. *A Snake Goddess Riding an Elephant*
Tibet, 18th century
Bronze; 12⅜ x 8⅞ in. (31.4 x 22.5 cm.)
Pan-Asian Collection

4. *Akbar Crossing a Bridge of Boats: Illustration*
to the Akbar-nama (History of Akbar).
India, Mughal style, c. 1590
Opaque watercolors on paper; 14 x 9 in.
(35.5 x 22.9 cm.)
Victoria and Albert Museum, London

5. *Battle Scene: Illustration to the*
Akbar-nama
India, Mughal style, c. 1590
Opaque watercolors on paper; 8½ in.
(21.6 cm.)
Seattle Art Museum, Gift of Mrs. John C. Atwood, Jr.

6. *Emperor Kumaragupta Hunting*
India, 5th century
Gold coin; diam: 11/16 in. (1.8 cm.)
Gift of Justin Dart and Anna Bing Arnold
M.77.55.24

7. *Prince Hunting Tiger from an Elephant*
India, Rajput Style, Kotah School,
18th century

Ink and charcoal on paper; 12⅞ x 8⅜ in.
(32.7 x 21.3 cm.)
Pan-Asian Collection

8. *Royal Riders on Elephant*
India, Tamilnadu, 13th century
Bronze; 1⅛ x 1½ in. (2.9 x 3.9 cm.)
Private Collection

9. *A King Riding an Elephant*
Iran, Minai Bowl, 13th century
Painted and glazed ceramic, 3¼ x 7½ in.
(8.2 x 19.1 cm.)
Purchased with Balch Fund
M.45.3.113

10. *A Sketch of an Elephant Hunt*
India, Rajput Style, Kotah School,
1775–1800
Ink on paper; 18 x 25¼ in.
(45.7 x 64.2 cm.)
Gift of Paul F. Walter
M.80.291.2

11. *Monsoon Season: From a* Baramasa
Series
India, Rajput Style, Kotah School, c. 1725
Opaque colors and gold on paper;
12¾ x 8⅜ in. (32.4 x 21.3 cm.)
Formerly The Nasli and Alice
Heeramaneck Collection
Museum Associates Purchase
M.71.1.25

12. *The Mad Elephant Nalgiri* (detail)
India, Andhra Pradesh, 2nd–3rd century
White limestone; height: 14¼ in.
(36.2 cm.)
Gift of The Ahmanson Foundation
M.72.50.3

13. *Triumph of St. Stephen*
Holland, Dirk Volkertz Coornhert
(1519–1590)
Engraving; 8½ x 10¼ in. (21.6 x 26.0 cm.)
Gift of Mrs. Irene Salinger
54.78.67

14. *The Return of the Errant Lover*
India, Rajput Style, Malwa School,

c. 1650
Opaque watercolors on paper;
8⁹/₁₆ x 5¾ in. (21.8 x 14.1 cm.)
Formerly The Nasli and Alice
Heeramaneck Collection
Museum Associates Purchase
M.71.1.16

15. *Indra and Sachi Riding the Divine Elephant Airavata*
India, Rajput Style, Amber School,
18th century
Opaque watercolors on paper;
10½ x 16¾ in. (26.6 x 42.5 cm.)
Indian Art Special Purposes Fund
M.74.102.4

16. *Indra on Airavata*
Thailand, Khmer Style, 13th century
Buff sandstone; 26½ x 55 in.
(67.3 x 139.7 cm.)
The Michael J. Connell Fund
M.75.104

17. *The Goddess Lakshmi Bathed by Elephants*
India, Orissa, 17th century
Brass; height: 9¼ in. (23.5 cm.)
Indian Art Special Purposes Fund
M.74.40.1

18. *A Priest Worshiping an Elephant*
Nepal, 17th century
Opaque watercolors on wood; 4½ x 10 in.
(11.9 x 25.4 cm.)
Private Collection

19. *King Vessantara Gives His White Elephant Away*
Thailand, 19th century
Opaque watercolors on cloth;
15½ x 15½ in. (39.4 x 39.4 cm.)
Gift of Margot and Hans Ries
M.76.112.20

20. *Vishnu Rescues Gajendra, the Elephant King*
India, Rajput Style, Kotah School, c. 1825
Ink and color washes on paper;

11¾ x 11 in. (29.9 x 27.9 cm.)
Gift of Paul F. Walter
M.76.149.5

21. *Elephant as an Auspicious Symbol: From a Jaina* Kalpasutra *Manuscript*
India, Gujarat, 16th century
Opaque watercolors on paper;
4½ x 3¼ in. (11.4 x 8.2 cm.)
Formerly The Nasli and Alice
Heeramaneck Collection
M.72.53.16

22. *Krishna Killing the Elephant Kuvalayapida*
India, Rajput Style, Guler School;
18th century
Opaque watercolors on paper;
6¼ x 10¼ in. (15.5 x 26 cm.)
Doris Wiener Gallery

23. *Mahishasura in the Guise of an Elephant Attacks the Goddess*
India, Rajput Style, Guler School, c. 1750
Opaque watercolors on paper;
6¾ x 10½ in. (17.2 x 26.6 cm.)
Purchased with Funds from
Christian Humann
M.74.14

24. *Buddha Taming the Mad Elephant Nalagiri*
India, Bihar, A.D. 1052
Opaque watercolors on palm-leaf;
2 x 2½ in. (5.1 x 6.4 cm.)
Formerly The Nasli and Alice
Heeramaneck Collection
Museum Associates Purchase
M.72.1.1

25. *Fever Attacking an Elephant*
India, Rajput Style, Mewar School,
18th century
Opaque watercolors on paper;
11¹¹⁄₁₆ x 10¼ in. (29.7 x 26 cm.)
Paul F. Walter Collection

26. *Lohan on Elephant*
China, 17th century
Wood with traces of lacquer and

gildings; height: 19 in. (48.2 cm.)
Robert A. Moore Collection

27. *Foreign Groom on Elephant*
China, 17th century
Jade; 2½ x 4 in. (6.4 x 10.1 cm.)
Asian Art Museum of San Francisco
The Avery Brundage Collection

28. *Elephants Sporting in Water*
India, Rajput Style, 17th century
Opaque watercolors on paper;
4½ x 7⅞ in. (11.9 x 20 cm.)
Pan-Asian Collection

29. *Elephant*
North India, 3rd century B.C.
Terracotta; height: 9½ in. (24.1 cm.)
Paul F. Walter Collection

30. *Forepart of an Elephant*
Sri Lanka, 2nd century B.C.
Terracotta; 7¾ x 5½ in. (19.7 x 14.0 cm.)
Mr. & Mrs. Lawrence Phillips Collection

31. *Toy Elephant*
North India, 2nd century B.C.
Terracotta; 4¼ x 2⅞ in. (10.8 x 7.3 cm.)
Private Collection

32. *Elephant with Riders*
India, Deccan, 18th century
Terracotta; height: 5¹¹⁄₁₆ in. (15.1 cm.)
Nasli and Alice Heeramaneck Collection
L.69.24.243

33. *Calf Elephant*
India, Tamilnadu, 13th century
Bronze; 2 x 3⁹⁄₁₆ in. (5.1 x 9.6 cm.)
Formerly The Nasli and Alice
Heeramaneck Collection
Museum Associates Purchase
M.72.1.18

34. *Elephant with Mahout*
Thailand, Sawankhaloke,
14th–15th century
Stoneware with celadon glaze;
5¼ x 5½ in. (13.4 x 14.0 cm.)
Private Collection

35. *Candlestick with Elephant and Riders*
India, Chamba, 17th century
Bronze; 15¼ x 11 in. (38.8 x 28.8 cm.)
Dr. and Mrs. J. Pollock Collection

36. *Tile with Elephant*
Sri Lanka, 10th–12th century
Terracotta; 11¾ x 5½ in.
(29.8 x 13.9 cm.)
Anonymous Gift
M.78.131.1

37. *Tile with Elephant*
Sri Lanka, 10th–12th century
Terracotta with polychrome; 6¼ x 4¾ in.
(16.0 x 12.1 cm.)
Mr. & Mrs. Lawrence Phillips Collection

38. *Elephant*
Indonesia, East Java, 13th–14th century
Terracotta; 15 x 25 in. (38.1 x 63.5 cm.)
The Vallin Galleries, Wilton, Ct.

39. *Throne Back from an Image of Tara*
India, Sirpur, c. 800
Bronze; height: 15 in. (38.1 cm.)
Nasli and Alice Heeramaneck Collection
L.69.24.277

40. *Elephant*
Sri Lanka, date unknown
Bronze; 2⅛ x 3⅞ in. (5.4 x 9.8 cm.)
Private Collection

41. *Elephant*
Iran, 13th–14th century
Grey stone; 2⅝ x 3½ in. (6.6 x 8.9 cm.)
The Nasli M. Heeramaneck Collection
Gift of Joan Palevsky
M.73.5.302

42. *Pot in the Shape of an Elephant*
Cambodia; 12th–13th century
Stoneware; 16½ x 17 in. (41.9 x 43.2 cm.)
Pan-Asian Collection

43. *An Elephant Fight*
India, Rajput style, Kotah School, c. 1850
Ink and color washes on paper;
12¹³⁄₁₆ x 20½ in. (32.6 x 52.1 cm.)

Gift of Paul F. Walter
M.77.154.23

44. *An Elephant Fight*
India, Rajput Style, Kotah School, 1800
Ink, charcoal and color wash on paper,
14³/₈ x 22³/₁₆ in. (36.5 x 56.4 cm.)
Gift of Paul F. Walter
M.77.154.19

45. *Taming the Elephant "Chanchal"*
India, Rajput Style, Mewar School;
dated 1760
Opaque watercolors on paper; 5 x 7 in.
(12.7 x 17.8 cm.)
Gift of Mr. and Mrs. Frank Neustatter
M.72.24

46. *Elephant on a Summer Day*
India, Rajput Style, Bundi School, c. 1750
Opaque watercolors on paper
Prince of Wales Museum, Bombay

47. *Kanhra Ragini*
India, Rajput Style, Marwar School;
c. 1750
Opaque watercolors on paper;
14⁵/₈ x 12 in. (37.2 x 30.5 cm.)
Indian Art Special Purposes Fund
M.81.29

48. *Worship of Ganesa*
Frontispiece of a Manuscript
India, Rajput Style, Mewar School,
c. 1725
Opaque watercolors on paper;
10 x 16³/₈ in. (25.5 x 42.9 cm.)
Mrs. Leroy Davidson Collection

49. *Ganesa*
India, Kashmir; 11th century
Bronze; 6 x 3½ in. (15.2 x 8.8 cm.)
Gift of Christian Humann
M.78.130.2

50. *Ganesa*
India, Kashmir, 11th century
Green stone; 7¼ x 5¼ in.
(18.4 x 13.3 cm.)
Beverly Coburn Collection

51. *Ganesa Dancing with His Spouse*
Nepal, 17th century
Colors on wood; 4½ x 10 in.
(11.4 x 25.5 cm.)
Private Collection

52. *Ganesa Seated on His Rat*
India, Himachal Pradesh; 12th century
Bronze; height: 4⁵/₈ in. (11 cm.)
Peter and Susan Strauss Collection

53. *Dancing Ganesa*
Nepal, 12th century
Bronze; height: 3½ in. (8.9 cm.)
Bob and Amy Poster Collection
Photograph by Scott Hyde

54. *Ganesa*
Indonesia, East Java; 15th century
Chalk stone; height: 3¼ in. (8.3 cm.)
Mrs. Roslynd Singer Collection

55. *Ganesa*
Indonesia, Central Java;
9th–10th century
Bronze; height: 5¾ in. (13.7 cm.)
Pan-Asian Collection

56. *Ganesa*
India, Himachal Pradesh; 16th century
Wood; 10 x 12¼ in. (25.4 x 31.1 cm.)
Mrs. Roslynd Singer Collection

57. *Ganesa*
Cambodia, 12th century
Bronze; height: 5¼ in. (14.0 cm.)
Pan-Asian Collection

58. *Ganesa*
Cambodia, 12th century
Bronze, height: 3⅛ in. (7.9 cm.)
Gift of Mr. and Mrs. Michael Phillips
M.79.189.5

59. *Embracing Elephant-headed Deities*
(Kangi-ten)
Japan, 15th century
Bronze; height: 4¾ in. (12.1 cm.)
Mrs. Roslynd Singer Collection

60. *Parvati Nursing Ganesa*
North India, 19th century
Opaque watercolors on paper; 15 x 11 in.
(38.1 x 27.9 cm.)
Mr. and Mrs. John G. Ford Collection

61. *The Holy Family*
India, Rajput Style, Mandi School; c. 1800
Opaque watercolors on paper;
9¾ x 7¾ in. (24.7 x 19.7 cm.)
Edwin Binney 3rd Collection

62. *Leaf of 'Barberini Diptych' Showing a*
Triumphant Justinian
Byzantine, c. 540
Ivory
The Louvre, Paris
Reproduced from E. Kitzinger,
Byzantine Art in The Making,
Harvard University Press

63. *Comb with Dancing Female*
Sri Lanka, 18th century
Ivory with polychrome; 6³/₈ x 4⅞ in.
(16.2 x 12.4 cm.)
Don and Corky Whitaker Collection

64. *Comb with Birds*
Sri Lanka, 18th century
Ivory, 4¾ x 3³/₈ in. (12.1 x 8.6 cm.)
Mr. and Mrs. Lawrence Phillips
Collection

65. *Comb with the God Vishnu*
Nepal, 17th century
Ivory; 3⅝ x 3 in. (9.2 x 7 cm.)
Gift of Don and Corky Whitaker
M.80.232.1

66. *Comb with Lion*
South India, 18th century
Ivory; 6³/₈ x 1⅝ in. (16.2 x 4.1 cm.)
Private Collection

67. *A Pair of Sandals*
India, 18th century
Ivory; 2½ x 9 in. (6.3 x 22.8 cm.)
Indian Art Special Purposes Fund
M.81.155a,b

68. *Cylindrical Box*
Sri Lanka, 18th century
Ivory; 5½ x 1¾ in. (13.9 x 4.4 cm.)
Gift of Don and Corky Whitaker
M.80.232.3

69. *Chest*
North India, 17th century
Ivory; 15 x 21¼ x 14¾ in.
(38.0 x 54.0 x 37.5 cm.)
Mr. and Mrs. Michael Douglas Collection

70. *Chest* (detail)
North India, 17th century
Wood with ivory inlay; 13 x 22 x 15 in.
(33 x 55.9 x 38.1 cm.)
Mr. and Mrs. Alan C. Balch Collection
M.73.47.1

71. *Panel with Courtiers*
India, Deccan, 17th century
Ivory; 2⅛ x 9⅝ in. (5.3 x 24.4 cm.)
Indian Art Special Purposes Fund
M.75.59.2

72. *Panel with Courtiers*
India, Deccan, 17th century
Ivory; 2⅛ x 9⅝ in. (5.3 x 24.4 cm.)
Edwin Binney 3rd Collection

73. *A Nobleman with Attendant*
India, Orissa, 17th century
Ivory; 7¼ x 3¼ in. (18.4 x 8.2 cm.)
Gift of Don and Corky Whitaker
M.80.232.5

74. *Lady Playing with Ball*
India, Orissa, 17th century
Ivory; 5⅝ x 3⅜ in. (14.3 x 8.5 cm.)
Gift of Don and Corky Whitaker
M.80.232.6

75. *Lovers in a Pavilion*
India, Orissa, 14th century
Ivory; 3⅞ x 2⅜ in. (9.5 x 6.0 cm.)
Pan-Asian Collection

76. *Lovers in a Pavilion*
India, Orissa, c. 1700
Ivory; 8 x 1 in. (20.3 x 2.1 cm.)
Gift of Paul F. Walter
M.72.107

77. *Rearing Lion*
India, Orissa, 17th century
Ivory; 4⅞ x 3 in. (12.3 x 7.6 cm.)
Gift of Don and Corky Whitaker
M.80.232.2

78. *Throne Leg in the Form of Rearing Lion*
North India, 17th century
Ivory; height: 5¾ in. (14.6 cm.)
Gift of Don and Corky Whitaker
M.80.232.7

79. *Throne Leg with Lion and Elephant Motif*
India, Orissa, 16th century
Ivory; height: 16 in. (40.7 cm.)
Seattle Art Museum
Eugene Fuller Memorial Collection

80. *Corner Pieces of a Throne with Lion, Elephant and Cherubs*
India, Orissa, 15th century
Ivory; 3⅞ x 3⅜ in. (9.8 x 8.5 cm.)
Gift of Don and Corky Whitaker
M.80.232.8a-d.

81. *Throne Leg with Rearing Lion Motif*
India, Orissa, 17th century
Ivory; height: 8 in. (20.0 cm.)
Los Angeles County Funds
M.70.2

82. *Panel with Composite Animals*
Western India, 18th century
Ivory with colors; 5½ x 11⅞ in.
(14 x 30.2 cm.)
Gift of Mrs. Marilyn M. Grounds
M.80.226.1

83. *Dagger with a Ram Handle*
India, 17th century
Ivory handle, 7½ x ¾ in. (19.1 x 9 cm.)
Mrs. Leroy Davidson Collection

84. *Sword* (kris) *with Demoness*
Indonesia, Bali, 19th century
Ivory handle; height: 4 in. (10.2 cm.)
Pan-Asian Collection

85. *Gunpowder Horn*
North India, 17th century
Ivory; 8 x 1½ in. (20.3 x 3.8 cm.)
Don and Corky Whitaker Collection

86. *Female Archer with Hunters*
India, Deccan, 17th century
Ivory; height: 8¼ in. (21 cm.)
Indian Art Special Purposes Fund
M.75.80

87. *Cylindrical Base with Dancing Peacock*
India, Deccan, c. 1700
Ivory; height: 3⅝ in. (9.2 cm.)
Private Collection

88. *Portrait of an Englishman*
India, c. 1800
Ivory; height: 3⁹/₁₆ in. (9 cm.)
Private Collection

89. *Portrait of an Indian*
India, c. 1800
Ivory; 3⁹/₁₆ in. (9 cm.)
Private Collection

90. *Portrait of a Nobleman*
Sri Lanka, Kandy, 18th century
Ivory; height: 8½ in. (21.6 cm.)
Gift of Anna Bing Arnold
M.81.35

91. *Child Krishna Fluting*
North India, c. 1900
Ivory; height: 8¹/₁₆ in. (20.4 cm.)
Pan-Asian Collection

92. *Yasoda Swinging Krishna*
South India, 17th century
Ivory; 5½ x 2⅜ in. (13.9 x 6 cm.)
Don and Corky Whitaker Collection

93. *Vishnu Adored by Serpents*
Nepal, 18th century
Ivory; 2¾ x 3⅛ in. (6.9 x 7.9 cm.)
Don and Corky Whitaker Collection

94. *Mara's Attendants*
India, Kashmir, 8th century
Ivory with pigments; 2½ x 1¼ in.

(6.4 x 3.2 cm.)
Don and Corky Whitaker Collection

*95. *Buddha Visited by Indra*
India, Kashmir, 8th century
Ivory with pigments
G. K. Kanoria Collection, India

96. *Section of a Tusk Carved with Buddhas*
Burma, 17th century
Ivory; height: 25½ in. (65 cm.)
Paul F. Walter Collection

97. *Buddha*
Sri Lanka, Kandy, 17th century
Ivory with polychrome; height: 13¾ in.
(34.9 cm.)
Julian Wright Bequest
M.80.58

98. *Buddha in Meditation*
Sri Lanka, Kandy, 18th century
Ivory; height: 1⅝ in. (4.1 cm.)
Gift of Mr. and Mrs. Michael Phillips
M.80.228.15

99. *Bodhisattvas*
Sino-Tibetan, 14th century
Ivory with polychrome; height: 12½ in.
(31.9 cm.)
Pan-Asian Collection

100. *Daka or Za-byed (The Devourer)*
Sino-Tibetan, 16th century
Ivory; height: 6 in. (15.2 cm.)
Pan-Asian Collection

101. *Padmasambhava*
Tibet, 17th century
Ivory, 5½ x 3½ (13.9 x 8.9 cm.)
Don and Corky Whitaker Collection

102. *Phur-bu (Ritual Dagger)*
Tibet, 17th century
Ivory; height: 8½ in. (21.6 cm.)
Mrs. Leroy Davidson Collection

103. *Stupa*
Sri Lanka, Kandy, 18th century
Ivory with colors; height: 8⅛ in.
(20.6 cm.)

Gift of Mrs. Beverly Coburn
M.78.101.2

104. *Fan*
Sri Lanka, Kandy, 18th century
Ivory handle; assembled height: 35¼ in.
(89.2 cm.)
Mr. and Mrs. Lawrence Phillips
Collection

105. *Crucifixion*
India, Goa, 17th century
Ivory; height: 14 in. (35.6 cm.)
Private Collection

106. *Madonna and Child*
India, Goa, 18th century
Ivory; height: 4⅞ in. (12.4 cm.)
Private Collection

107. *The Virgin Mary*
India, Goa, 18th century
Ivory; height: 7⅛ in. (18.2 cm.)
Mrs. Leroy Davidson Collection

108. *St. John*
India, Goa, 17th century
Ivory; height: 4⅛ in. (10.5 cm.)
Mrs. Leroy Davidson Collection

Index